## CONTRIBUTORS AND CONSULTANTS

# THE
# GOLDEN BOOK
# ENCYCLOPEDIA

## VOLUME XI—NAVY TO PARASITES

In Sixteen Accurate, Fact-filled Volumes Dramatically Illustrated
with More Than 6,000 Color Pictures

THE ONLY ENCYCLOPEDIA FOR YOUNG GRADE-SCHOOL CHILDREN

ACCURATE AND AUTHORITATIVE

ENTERTAININGLY WRITTEN AND ILLUSTRATED TO
MAKE LEARNING AN ADVENTURE

## by Bertha Morris Parker

*Formerly of the Laboratory Schools, University of Chicago*
*Research Associate, Chicago Natural History Museum*

GOLDEN PRESS · NEW YORK

**THIRD PRINTING, 1960**
© Copyright 1959 by Golden Press, Inc. Designed and produced by Artists and
Writers Press, Inc. Printed in the U.S.A. by Western Printing and Lithographing
Company. Published by Golden Press, Inc., Rockefeller Center, New York 20, N.Y.

Illustrations from GOLDEN BOOKS, published by Golden Press, Inc., New York,© 1946,1949,
1950, 1951, 1952, 1953, 1954, 1955, 1956, 1957, by Golden Press, Inc.; and from the Basic
Science Education Series (Unitext), published by Row, Peterson and Company, Evanston, Illi-
nois, © 1941, 1944, 1947, 1949, 1952, 1957, 1958, 1959 by Row, Peterson and Company.

Early warships had to be rowed.

**NAVY** The story of navies begins long ago. The ancient Egyptians, Cretans, Phoenicians, Persians, and Greeks all had warships. But their fighting fleets were very different from the navies of today.

The early warships had to be rowed from place to place. Today some naval vessels are driven by atomic power.

The early naval battles were really hand to hand battles. The ships came close together, and the men fought with swords and spears. One ship might sink an enemy ship by ramming it.

Twenty-two hundred years ago, Roman war vessels had machines for throwing stones and darts The machines were operated by springs. During the Middle Ages warships hurled "Greek fire," a mixture of chemicals, on enemy ships to burn them.

By the end of the 1500's it was possible to have guns on warships. Modern warships have long-range guns and rocket-launching devices. Torpedoes and mines are used in modern naval fighting, too.

In early days a few ships, all of about the same kind, made up a fleet. A strong

First Ironclad Battleships (1862)

navy of today has hundreds of vessels of many different kinds.

The "queens" of modern navies are the huge airplane carriers, or flattops. The biggest flattops have room for more than 100 fighter planes. Other fighting ships are battleships, cruisers, destroyers, submarines, PT boats (patrol torpedo boats), mine layers, mine sweepers, and submarine chasers.

There must be transport ships, too, to carry troops and supplies to where they are needed. There are helper, or auxiliary, ships such as hospital ships, tenders, and oilers.

PT Boats of World War II

Atomic-powered Submarine

And there are landing ships for carrying men from big transport vessels to shore.

There have been many famous naval battles in the history of the world. Among them are the Battle of Salamis, the battle between the "Bonhomme Richard" and the "Serapis," and the battle between the "Monitor" and the "Merrimac." (See ARMADA; GREECE; JONES, JOHN PAUL; MONITOR AND THE MERRIMAC; OLD IRONSIDES; SHIPS; SUBMARINES; U. S. ARMED FORCES; WORLD WAR I.)

Under Hitler, German boys and girls
were organized into youth groups.

**NAZIS** After World War I Germany became a republic. The people elected a president just as the United States does. For a time the new German republic was prosperous. But then everything began going wrong. There was a depression in the United States and in most of the rest of the world. It was especially bad in Germany. When the Germans were greatly discouraged, a new leader appeared. He was Adolf Hitler, the head of a party called the National Socialists. The members of this party were called the Nazis for short.

Hitler and the Nazis became very powerful. Their song was "Today We Own Germany, Tomorrow the World." Their flag with its swastika waved everywhere in Germany. The Nazis started World War II by marching into Poland. In a large part of the world "Nazi" soon became one of the most hated of all words. (See DICTATORS; GERMANY; WORLD WAR II.)

**NEAR EAST** The name "Near East" is often used for the lands at the eastern end of the Mediterranean Sea. The Near East has played a very important part in the history of the world. Down through the centuries it has been a bridge between Asia to the east and Europe and Africa to the west. The region was the homeland of the ancient Egyptians, Babylonians, Assyrians, Hittites, Persians, and Hebrews. By way of the Greeks and Romans, much of their civilization came to Europe and then to the Americas.

The Near East is the birthplace of three great religions — Judaism, Islam, and Christianity. Another great gift of the region to the world is the alphabet.

Over 95,000,000 people now live in the Near East. More than half of them speak Arabic. Other important languages in the area are Turkish, Persian, and Hebrew. Some small groups speak other languages such as Aramaic and Kurdish.

In the 8th century almost all the people of the Near East became Moslems — followers of Islam. Today most of the people are Moslems, but there are some Christians and Jews.

Although many millions of the people of the Near East are both Moslems and Arabs, the region is broken up into many countries. One part of the Near East got the name of the Fertile Crescent. It is a crescent of land curving from the shores of the Mediterranean over to and down the valleys of the Tigris and Euphrates rivers. The Fertile Crescent is now divided among Israel, Lebanon, Jordan, Syria, and Iraq. To the north and east of the Fertile Crescent are the bigger countries of Turkey and Iran. In the Arabian Peninsula we find large Saudi Arabia and small Yemen, Aden, Oman, Qatar, Bahrein, and Kuwait. Egypt is in northeast Africa. In 1958 Egypt and Syria joined to form the United Arab Republic.

Much of the land in the region is desert. Only a very small part of the land can be farmed. Most of the farmland is irrigated. Besides the deserts and farmlands there are grazing lands. Many of the people of the grazing lands are nomads. Life for the nomads has not changed much for several thousand years.

Although farmland is scarce, about half of all the people of the Near East are farmers. Modern ways of farming are being used in some places. In other places centuries-old ways are still followed.

There are several large cities in the Near East. The largest is Cairo, in Egypt. Other cities of over half a million people are Teheran in Iran, Alexandria in Egypt, Istanbul in Turkey, and Baghdad in Iraq. These cities are chiefly trading centers. Not much manufacturing goes on.

The great riches of the region are its oil fields. It is the greatest oil exporting region of the world. The chief oil-producing

Pipelines carry Near East oil to port cities.

countries are Iran, Iraq, Kuwait, Saudi Arabia, Bahrein, and Qatar. Long pipelines carry oil from some of the fields to the Mediterranean coast. From there tankers carry it to the world's markets. Other tankers pick up oil from the shores of the Persian Gulf. Because of the great stores of oil the rest of the world is very much interested in what goes on in the Near East. (See ALPHABET; ASIA; BABYLONIA; EGYPT; IRAN; IRAQ; ISRAEL; NOMADS; PERSIA; TURKEY.)

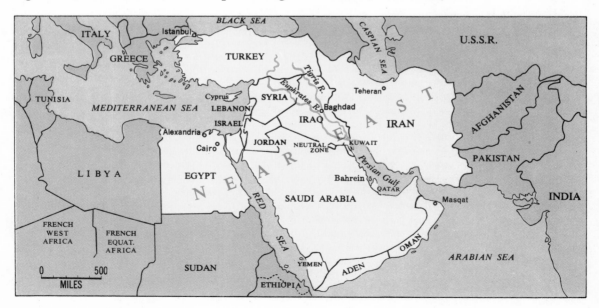

**NEBRASKA** This central state stretches from rolling prairie in the east to the Rocky Mountains in the west. Its name comes from an Indian word, *Nebrathka*, meaning "river in the flatness." The Indians gave this name to the Platte River, which flows through flat land from the Wyoming border to the Missouri River.

Nebraska is called the Cornhusker State. It is a leading farm state, and its biggest crop is corn. The farms differ from one part of the state to another. The eastern prairie farms are part of the corn-and-livestock region called the Corn Belt. The western farms of Nebraska lie on the Great Plains. Many of them are cattle ranches with thousands of acres of grazing land. The southern farms produce much wheat, like the nearby Kansas farms. Cattle, corn, hogs, and wheat are the big money-makers in Nebraska.

Omaha is the leading meat-packing city in the United States. Another nickname for Nebraska is Beef State. Farmers now haul most of their animals to market in trucks. Many farmers who used to ship their livestock to Chicago now find it cheaper and easier to drive their trucks to Omaha. In addition to its stockyards and meat-packing plants, Omaha has large dairy plants and flour mills. This busy river city has over 250,000 people. Lincoln, the capital, Grand Island, and Hastings are other trade and manufacturing cities. Each has less than 100,000 people.

The pioneers and later settlers deserve much credit for their work in developing Nebraska. Some pioneers from covered-wagon days stayed to become farmers on the prairies of eastern Nebraska. Settlement was speeded up after Congress passed the Homestead Act in 1862. This act made it possible to gain 160 acres of farmland at very little cost.

The railroads, pushing westward in the 1870's and 1880's, encouraged settlers to come to Nebraska. Many German as well as American pioneers arrived on the new

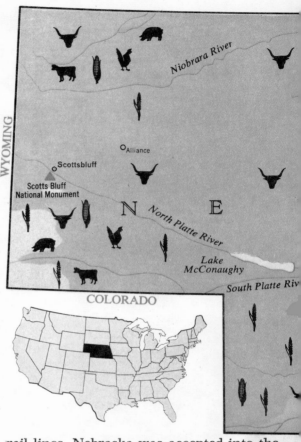

rail lines. Nebraska was accepted into the Union as the 37th state in 1867.

The pioneers on the prairies felt the need for trees. They built their first homes of sod and got along as best they could without much wood. Early settlers sent east for seedlings. They planted them along the fence rows and about their homes to form windbreaks and to hold moisture in the soil. J. Sterling Morton settled in Nebraska in 1855 and soon started a tree planting program. It was he who in 1872 founded Arbor Day.

The pioneers saw the need for irrigation, too. The rains are very uncertain. The first irrigation ditch was dug before Nebraska became a state. At least 1,000,000 acres of Nebraska's farmlands are now irrigated. Some farmers have electric pumps that pump well water to huge sprays placed in their fields.

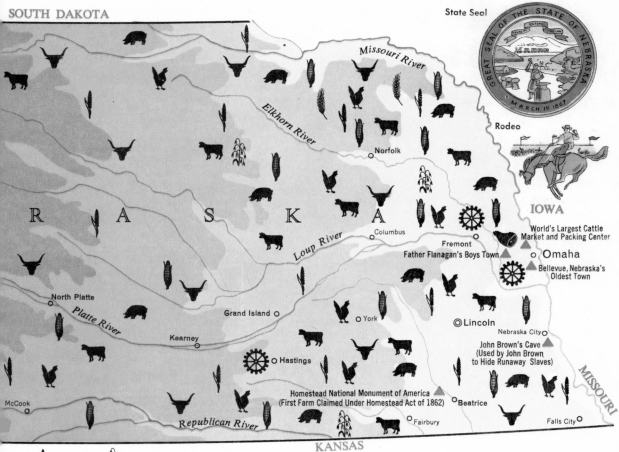

SOUTH DAKOTA

State Seal

Missouri River

Elkhorn River

Norfolk

Rodeo

IOWA

Loup River

Columbus

Fremont

World's Largest Cattle
Market and Packing Center

Father Flanagan's Boys Town

Omaha

Bellevue, Nebraska's
Oldest Town

North Platte

Platte River

Grand Island

York

Lincoln

Nebraska City

Kearney

Hastings

John Brown's Cave
(Used by John Brown
to Hide Runaway Slaves)

McCook

Homestead National Monument of America
(First Farm Claimed Under Homestead Act of 1862)

Beatrice

MISSOURI

Republican River

Fairbury

Falls City

KANSAS

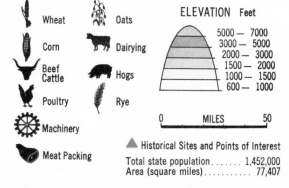

Wheat          Oats

Corn           Dairying

Beef           Hogs
Cattle

Poultry        Rye

Machinery

Meat Packing

ELEVATION  Feet

5000 — 7000
3000 — 5000
2000 — 3000
1500 — 2000
1000 — 1500
600 — 1000

0        MILES        50

▲ Historical Sites and Points of Interest

Total state population....... 1,452,000
Area (square miles).......... 77,407

The United States Government's project
in the Missouri River Basin will help a
large number of people in Nebraska. There
will be less danger of flood damage after
very heavy rains. The rivers will be better
able to carry freight. And there will be
more water for irrigation. Nebraska will
have much more land to cultivate. Its population will probably increase. Now 15th in
size, it ranks 33rd in population.

State Flag

State Capitol

State Bird:
Western
Meadowlark

Wheat
Combine

State Flower:
Goldenrod

The Great Nebula in Orion's Sword

**NEBULAS** The word "nebula" comes from a Latin word that means "cloud." But a nebula is not like any of the clouds that float across our sky. These clouds are made of tiny drops of water or bits of ice. A nebula is made of star dust or gas.

In the night sky the nebulas we can see look like tiny fuzzy patches of light. Through a telescope we find out that they are not all the same shape. One, for example, is shaped like a ring. These nebulas shine, scientists think, because they reflect light from stars near by.

There are some nebulas that do not shine. They are dark. There are no bright stars near by to light them up. We know about them only because they shut off the view of what is beyond them out in space.

One of the best-known of the bright nebulas is in Orion. Orion is the brightest group of stars in the sky. The ancient Greeks saw in this group of stars the picture of a hunter. The hunter wore a sword in his belt. The nebula of Orion is located in Orion's sword.

The Horsehead nebula is one of the best-known dark nebulas. It also is in Orion. Another well-known dark nebula is in the Milky Way. It is called the Coal Sack. (See ASTRONOMY; CLOUDS; MILKY WAY; SKY; STARS.)

**NEGRO** Scientists divide all the races of people into three groups. These three groups are often called the white races, the yellow races, and the black races. Better names for them are Caucasoid, Mongoloid, and Negroid. Negroes, as anyone would guess, are in the Negroid group.

The native home of the Negro is in Africa. There are many different groups of Negroes there. They speak many languages, and have many different customs. As a rule they have brown or black skin, kinky black hair, dark-brown eyes, broad noses, and thick lips. They differ greatly in size. Some are seven feet tall. Others seldom grow to be more than five feet tall.

Some of the Negroes of Africa still live very simply, much as their ancestors did centuries ago. They get much of their food by hunting and fishing. But many are now farmers, and many work for Europeans

Gaseous Nebula in Orion

who have settled in Africa. Some are doctors, nurses, and teachers.

The Negroes have spread from Africa to many other lands. Columbus, it is said, had a Negro in the crew of one of his ships. Some of the other men who explored the New World—Balboa, Cortes, and Pizarro—had Negroes among their men. After settlement of the New World began, most of the Negroes who reached the Americas were brought as slaves. Before the War between the States there were many Negro slaves in the Southern states. That war was brought on partly because the North and the South did not agree about slavery. Abraham Lincoln's Emancipation Proclamation freed all the slaves of the South.

Even after the slaves were freed, they did not have much chance to move forward. Many ways of earning a living were closed to them. It was not easy for a Negro to get an education. But now the chances of getting a good education are far better, and Negroes have become famous in many fields. They have been helped in their struggle upward by such great Negro teachers and scientists as Booker T. Washington and George Washington Carver.

Today many records in sports are held by American Negroes. They have made a great name for themselves in boxing, baseball, and basketball. Many popular entertainers are Negroes. There are distinguished Negro ministers, doctors, lawyers, teachers, musicians, and writers. Negroes are helping to prove that scientists are right in saying that no one race is more capable than other races.

One country of Africa was founded by Negroes who returned to Africa from America. That country is Liberia. Another part of Africa with a population almost entirely Negro has recently become an independent country. It is Ghana. Many of the Negroes of Africa, however, live in colonies belonging to countries of Europe. (See CARVER, GEORGE WASHINGTON; RACES OF MANKIND; WASHINGTON, BOOKER T.)

African Native Carving a Stool

Cotton Picking on a Southern Plantation

Entertainers

Scientist

Civic Leader

Nurse

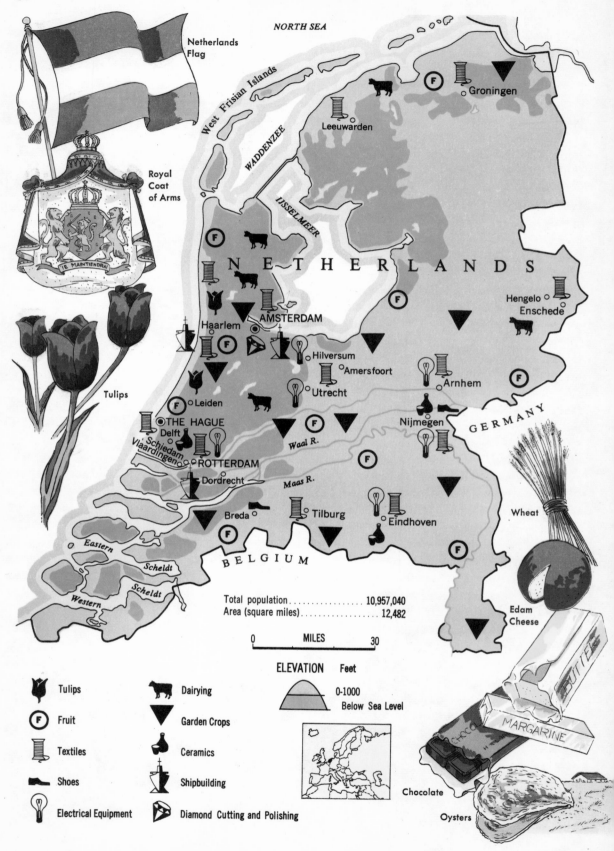

NORTH SEA

Netherlands
Flag

West Frisian Islands

WADDENZEE

IJSSELMEER

Royal
Coat
of Arms

IE MAINTIENDRAI

N E T H E R L A N D S

Groningen

Leeuwarden

Hengelo
Enschede

Haarlem

AMSTERDAM

Hilversum

Amersfoort

Arnhem

Utrecht

Leiden

THE HAGUE
Delft

Nijmegen

Schiedam
Vlaardingen

ROTTERDAM

Dordrecht

Waal R.

Maas R.

GERMANY

Tulips

Breda

Tilburg

Eindhoven

Wheat

Eastern

Scheldt

BELGIUM

Edam
Cheese

Western

Scheldt

Total population . . . . . . . . . . . . . . . . . 10,957,040
Area (square miles) . . . . . . . . . . . . . . . . 12,482

0      MILES      30

ELEVATION   Feet

0-1000
Below Sea Level

Tulips

Fruit

Textiles

Shoes

Electrical Equipment

Dairying

Garden Crops

Ceramics

Shipbuilding

Diamond Cutting and Polishing

Chocolate

MARGARINE

BUTTER

CHOCO

Oysters

**NETHERLANDS** The small country called the Netherlands, with its front door on the North Sea, is a low, or "nether," country. It is thickly settled by millions of people in towns and on farmlands.

The Netherlands was one of the first countries of Europe to recover prosperity after World War II. The Dutch have suffered from many wars. Their lowlands have no mountain barriers to keep out invading armies. Great rivers, like the Rhine, that flow through the Netherlands to reach the sea have furnished easy routes for invaders. Once long ago a Dutch army fought on skates to defeat an enemy. At times the Dutch have opened sea walls to flood out invaders. They have said, "Better a drowned land than a lost land."

The oldest, fiercest enemy of the Netherlands, however, has been the sea. Behind the coastal sand dunes, about half of the Netherlands lies below sea level. Long ago this half was only swamps and small lakes. A few fishermen lived on islands there.

The Dutch won many battles against the sea. They built strong dikes along the dunes. They drained water from wet land into canals and rivers. First pumps run by windmills and later electric pumps were used. Both kinds are still at work. In this drained land, or "polders," there now are pastures and fields of grain, potatoes, and sugar beets. Many tulips and other flowers are raised to sell to other lands.

In a great storm in 1953 the Dutch lost some of their polders. Hundreds of people and thousands of farm animals were drowned. Many villages were ruined. But the brave people began at once to win the land back from the sea again.

Zuider Zee, an arm of the North Sea, once reached far down into the Netherlands. There is no longer a Zuider Zee. Dutch engineers, by building dikes, first changed this arm of the sea into a fresh-water lake called Lake Yssel. Now they have drained part of the lake away. On what was once sea bottom there are green pastures and dairy farms. The brick farmhouses are shaded with trees. Under one roof, in many cases, are the family rooms, winter stalls for the cows, and a room for making and storing cheese. Much milk is sent to factories to be made into milk powder, cheese, and milk chocolate. Netherlands milk products go all over the world.

Important as farming is in the Netherlands, more people make a living by manufacturing and trade than by farming. The country has a good location for buying raw materials and selling factory goods. The ocean highway is at its door. The great Rhine is a river road to thickly-settled Germany and to Switzerland and France. Factories ranging from little wooden shoe workshops to steel mills and shipyards are scattered throughout the country.

The chief factory and trade cities are Amsterdam and Rotterdam. Amsterdam is the capital of the Netherlands. Many people there work in textile mills or cut and polish diamonds brought from Africa. In the huge harbor are many ships from lands overseas. Rotterdam is the doorway from the sea into the Rhine valley and is one of the greatest ports of Europe.

The people of little Netherlands are prosperous in spite of many hardships. (See CHEESE; DIKES AND LEVEES; NORTH SEA; RHINE RIVER; WORLD WAR II.)

Windmill Pumps    Tulip Raising    Modern High School

Dairying    Bicycle Travel

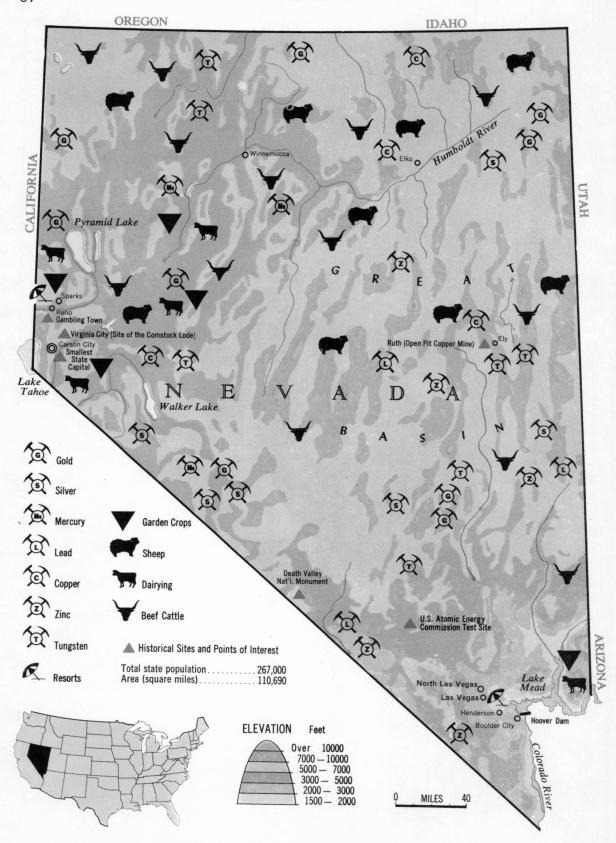

OREGON       IDAHO

CALIFORNIA

UTAH

Winnemucca

Elko

Humboldt River

G R E A T

Pyramid Lake

Sparks
Reno
Gambling Town
Virginia City (Site of the Comstock Lode)
Carson City
Smallest
State
Capital

Lake
Tahoe

N E V A D A

Walker Lake

B A S I N

Ruth (Open Pit Copper Mine)
Ely

ARIZONA

Death Valley
Nat'l. Monument

U.S. Atomic Energy
Commission Test Site

Lake
Mead

North Las Vegas
Las Vegas
Henderson
Boulder City
Hoover Dam

Colorado River

**Legend**

- G   Gold
- S   Silver
- Me   Mercury
- L   Lead
- C   Copper
- Z   Zinc
- T   Tungsten
- Resorts

- ▼   Garden Crops
- Sheep
- Dairying
- Beef Cattle
- ▲   Historical Sites and Points of Interest

Total state population . . . . . . . . . . . 267,000
Area (square miles) . . . . . . . . . . . . 110,690

ELEVATION   Feet

Over   10000
7000 — 10000
5000 — 7000
3000 — 5000
2000 — 3000
1500 — 2000

0   MILES   40

**NEVADA** Most of this large western state lies in the Great Basin. This high dry plateau is between the still higher Rockies on the east and the Sierra Nevada Mountains on the west. The name "Nevada" is a Spanish word meaning "snow-clad." Heavy winter snows fall on the Sierras and on the mountain ranges that cross the basin from north to south. But the "basin" is very dry. Less rain falls in a year in Nevada than in any other state in the country.

Only Alaska has fewer people and is more thinly settled than Nevada. Carson City is the smallest state capital.

Its nicknames, the "Sagebrush State" and the "Silver State," fit Nevada well. Much of the state is desert, with scattered sagebrush, cactus, and greasewood. Gold-seekers bound for California hurried over these desert lands. There were few settlers in Nevada before 1859. In that year two men hunting for gold in the western part of the Nevada country discovered a huge layer of silver. This vein was called the "Comstock Lode." Miners rushed in to open mines in this famous vein. Near the silver lode, Virginia City and other mining towns sprang up like magic.

Men began to search in other mountains of Nevada for precious metals. In 1873 they discovered the richest deposit of gold and silver in the world. This was called the "Big Bonanza." From it many people made great fortunes.

Before the coming of railroads to Nevada, miners used mules and covered wagons to bring in their supplies and to carry away the precious ores. One mining company used twelve camels from Asia. The camels served well in the Nevada desert.

In the 1860's, as the railroads reached Nevada, livestock ranches grew. Ranchers could ship cattle and sheep to markets by rail. But Nevada still had very few people when President Lincoln signed the proclamation making it a state in 1864.

Today, ranches and farms earn for the people of Nevada more than its mines. The valleys between the mountain chains are covered with bunch grass. There great herds of cattle and sheep graze well even in winter. But eight out of every ten acres of land belong to the United States Government. Ranchers must get permits and pay fees to use government lands for grazing. Livestock raising tops all other kinds of farming. Since 1900, irrigation has helped to change some desert areas into good farmlands. Since 1936, the great Hoover Dam on the Colorado River near Boulder City has helped to irrigate farms and bring electricity to part of Nevada.

Copper is the most valuable product of Nevada mines today. Zinc, gold, silver, and tungsten are important, too. Nevada's mines also yield uranium for producing atomic energy. A government atomic-testing center is in the desert. The smelting and refining of ores are about the only manufacturing industries. Reno is the chief center. New factories have started at Las Vegas and Boulder City and use power from Hoover Dam. Taking care of visitors, however, is the main work in both Reno and Las Vegas. Every year many people visit these two resorts.

Hoover Dam

Discovery of Comstock Lode

State Flower: Sagebrush

State Flag

Steer Roping

State Bird: Mountain Bluebird

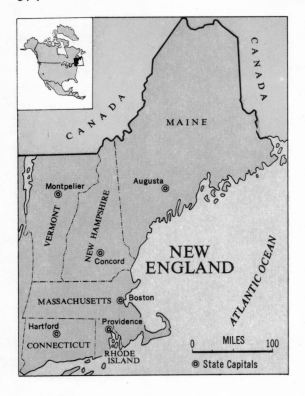

**NEW ENGLAND** The six states that make up the northeastern corner of the United States are called New England. Many of the early settlers there came from England. The land was named for the country they had left.

The map shows the six states that make up New England. Altogether they are smaller than Missouri. But they have more than twice as many people as there are in Missouri. A great many of the people of New England live in cities.

Much of New England is mountainous. The mountains are not very high, but their slopes are too steep for farming. Many are still covered with forests. Christmas trees are one of the important "crops" of Maine. Vermont is well known for the fine maple sirup that is made from the sap of its sugar maple trees. Some of the land that is level enough for farms is rocky and has rather poor soil. Farming was one of the chief occupations of the early settlers in New England. It had to be. But we can easily see that not a very big part of the ten million people that live in New England now could make their living by farming. There are, however, some good dairy farms, and the Connecticut Valley is famous for fine tobacco, Cape Cod for cranberries, and Maine for potatoes.

Fishing and trading and building ships give work to many New Englanders. Since very early days fleets of fishing vessels have gone out from New England ports and have brought back boatloads of fish. Trading vessels have left these ports to sail the seven seas. It is no wonder that shipbuilding is important there.

A few people make a living by quarrying. Vermont is well known for its granite and marble quarries.

New England has always been famous for its merchants. It has always been famous for its colleges. Taking care of tourists gives work to many New Englanders, too. Many people spend the summers along its coasts or in its mountains. Besides, thousands of tourists visit New England every year to see Lexington and Concord and other places that are important in early American history. There are many such places in New England.

Another very important way of earning a living in New England is working in factories. This part of the United States got an early start in manufacturing. It has no coal, no iron, and no great steel mills, but it has rivers with waterfalls that furnish water power for running electric power plants. This water power helps make weaving cloth easy. There are many great textile mills. New England's smaller factories make such things as tools, drugs, paper goods, carpets, and furniture.

Some of the farms of New England have been worn out and abandoned. Some of its factories have moved to other parts of the country. The states of New England are now seeking to attract new industries. (See CONNECTICUT; MAINE; MASSACHUSETTS; NEW HAMPSHIRE; RHODE ISLAND; VERMONT.)

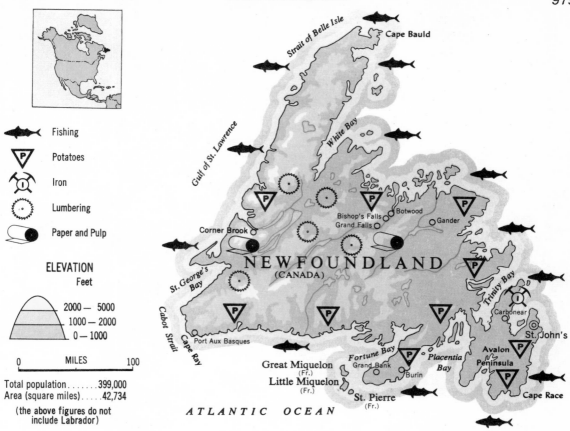

Fishing

Potatoes

Iron

Lumbering

Paper and Pulp

ELEVATION
Feet

2000 — 5000
1000 — 2000
0 — 1000

0          MILES          100

Total population . . . . . . . 399,000
Area (square miles) . . . . . 42,734

(the above figures do not
include Labrador)

**NEWFOUNDLAND** A province in Canada is like a state in the United States. Until 1948 Canada had nine provinces. Now there are ten. Newfoundland is the tenth.

Newfoundland is an island not far from the mouth of the great St. Lawrence River. It is about the size of Ohio. Before 1948 the island, along with Labrador, made up a separate part of the British Empire. But in 1948 its people voted to become one of the provinces of Canada.

Its name does not fit Newfoundland very well now. For John Cabot reached it and claimed it for England only five or six years after Columbus made his first trip to the New World.

The inner part of the island is mostly wilderness. Much of it is covered with forests. There are in all Newfoundland fewer people than there are in Columbus, Ohio. Most of the people live along the rocky coasts. Many of them make their living

fishing for cod. Newfoundland's codfish are shipped far and wide over the world. Newfoundland's forests furnish much wood for making paper. There are mines of several kinds, too.

Thousands of people visit Newfoundland each year. But most of them stay for only a few hours. They are on their way by plane to Europe or back to Canada and the United States. Newfoundland's Gander Airport is one of the world's great airports.

St. John's is Newfoundland's biggest city. It is on the southeastern coast.

Just reading the names on a map of Newfoundland makes one want to visit the island. Puddle Pond, Gulp Pond, and Sitdown Pond are three of the many little lakes. Main Topsail and Mizzen Topsail are high hills. Ireland's Eye, Heart's Delight, Come by Chance, St. Jones Without, and St. Jones Within are all villages. (See CANADA; FISHING.)

**NEW HAMPSHIRE** This part of New England was named New Hampshire by Captain John Mason. In 1629 he was granted the land between the Merrimack and the Piscataqua rivers by The Council for New England. The Council had received the land from King James I. Mason named his grant after Hampshire, his home in England.

New Hampshire is one of the small states. It is less than 100 miles across at its widest part and less than 200 miles from north to south. It is shaped somewhat like a triangle and is wedged in between Maine and Vermont with only about 19 miles of coast line on the Atlantic Ocean. The nickname for New Hampshire is "Granite State." Much of this very hard, beautiful stone is found in its mountains.

New Hampshire was one of the original thirteen colonies. The earliest colonists were fishermen from nearby Massachusetts. They settled near the Piscataqua River, at Dover and Portsmouth. Farmers soon came to settle the coastal plain and the valleys of the Merrimack and the Connecticut rivers. They found in these regions much fertile soil and plenty of rain, but very short seasons without frost. They grew hay and feed crops, and raised livestock. For 200 years most New Hampshire people were farmers.

Lumbering was important, too. As long ago as the 1670's New Hampshire was shipping much lumber across the sea. Out of their lumber the colonists themselves built many sailing ships for American and British traders. The tall pine trees in their forests made masts strong enough to weather Atlantic storms. In time some of the lumber was used for stagecoaches.

In the early 1800's, men set up small factories and mills in southern New Hampshire, near rivers to supply water power and to aid transportation. Many farmers turned to factory work. Among the earliest factories were cotton mills at Manchester and a shoe factory at Weare.

New Hampshire was the first colony to declare its independence from England and to set up its own government. In 1788, it joined the Union as the ninth state. Its capital is Concord.

Today, New Hampshire is still rather thinly settled. More than half of its people live in cities. But none of the cities are large. The principal factory and trade center is Manchester, with over 80,000 people. Other centers are Nashua, Concord, Portsmouth, and Berlin. In these cities there are shoe factories, cotton, rayon, and woolen mills, and lumber and paper mills.

The granite from the quarries is used for building stone. The Library of Congress at Washington, D. C., and many buildings and monuments throughout the United States are made of New Hampshire granite.

Now less than one in ten workers in New Hampshire are farmers. The main farm products are fruits, milk, and cattle.

Taking care of visitors gives work to many people. Ocean beaches, lakes, and the White Mountains make the state a pleasant vacation land in both winter and summer. The beauty of New Hampshire's hills and lakes will live, moreover, in the works of many writers. Joyce Kilmer wrote "Trees" while vacationing there. Many of Robert Frost's poems are about New Hampshire's woods and fields.

State Capitol

Lobster

Dairy Farming

Textile

Shoes

Poultry

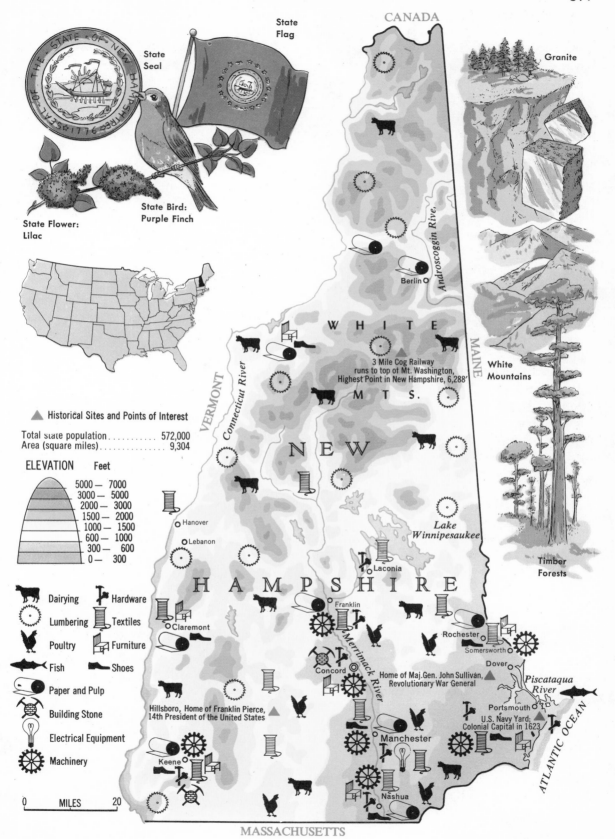

State Seal

State Flag

State Bird: Purple Finch

State Flower: Lilac

CANADA

Granite

Androscoggin River

Berlin

WHITE

MAINE

3 Mile Cog Railway runs to top of Mt. Washington, Highest Point in New Hampshire, 6,288'

White Mountains

M T S.

NEW

Timber Forests

▲ Historical Sites and Points of Interest

Total state population . . . . . . . . . . 572,000
Area (square miles) . . . . . . . . . . . . . 9,304

Lake Winnipesaukee

ELEVATION   Feet

| | |
|---|---|
| 5000 — | 7000 |
| 3000 — | 5000 |
| 2000 — | 3000 |
| 1500 — | 2000 |
| 1000 — | 1500 |
| 600 — | 1000 |
| 300 — | 600 |
| 0 — | 300 |

Connecticut River

VERMONT

Hanover

Lebanon

Laconia

HAMPSHIRE

Franklin

Rochester

Somersworth

Dover

Dairying       Hardware

Lumbering     Textiles

Poultry         Furniture

Fish            Shoes

Paper and Pulp

Building Stone

Electrical Equipment

Machinery

Claremont

Concord

Merrimack River

Home of Maj.Gen. John Sullivan, Revolutionary War General

Piscataqua River

Portsmouth

U.S. Navy Yard; Colonial Capital in 1623

Hillsboro, Home of Franklin Pierce, 14th President of the United States

ATLANTIC OCEAN

Keene

Manchester

0   MILES   20

Nashua

MASSACHUSETTS

# NEW JERSEY

**NEW JERSEY** This Middle Atlantic state is in the middle of the busiest part of the United States. The crowded New York City area sprawls across the Hudson River into northeastern New Jersey. The crowded Philadelphia area spreads across the Delaware River into southwestern New Jersey. There is an almost continuous belt of cities in the 90 miles across New Jersey between New York and Philadelphia — Newark, Jersey City, Trenton, Camden, and many others besides. Railroads, highways, and airlines cross New Jersey and meet the ocean liners at the port cities. The "Crossroads of the East" is a good name for this small, but important, state.

It is no wonder that New Jersey is, next to Rhode Island, the most thickly settled state in the country. Almost nine out of ten of its people live in its cities. But there are woods and marshes with very few people. Many people who live in New Jersey's cities go to New York or to Philadelphia every day to work. The cities of New Jersey have more room and in some ways are more attractive to live in than the two giant cities near by.

But thousands and thousands of the people who live in New Jersey's cities work in its own factories. Many of the factory buildings, especially in the New York area, are very new and have none of the ugly dirty look of old factory towns. Many modern chemical plants and research laboratories show that New Jersey is one of the leading states in the chemical industry. Making machinery, refining copper and petroleum, and making drugs and medicines are also important. Products from over 1,500 New Jersey factories and shops can be delivered overnight to millions of customers in 12 states.

New Jersey people are proud of the state's nickname, "The Garden State." Green lawns and flower gardens surround most city homes and the beautiful estates in the rolling, hilly section of northern New Jersey. The state is well known for the vegetables, poultry, and fruits raised on the coastal lowlands. Trucks and fast trains rush these products to markets, canneries, and quick-freeze plants.

New Jersey attracts many visitors. The Atlantic Coast for 120 miles is a sloping sandy beach, ideal for vacation resorts. Atlantic City with its famous boardwalk and hotels is the best known. The Delaware Water Gap, a gorge through the forested Kittatinny Mountains, and the Palisades, the rock cliffs along the Hudson, are among New Jersey's scenic attractions.

New Jersey was one of the original 13 colonies. In 1618 Dutch settlers came to its shores. Soon ships brought English and Swedish settlers. In 1664 England took possession of the colony and granted it to two Englishmen, Sir George Carteret and Lord Berkeley. They named their grant "New Jersey" after the island of Jersey, south of England, the birthplace of Sir George Carteret.

During the Revolutionary War, nearly 100 battles were fought in New Jersey. Here, General Washington and his army crossed the Delaware and fought the Battle of Trenton, which helped the Americans to win the war. In 1787 New Jersey became the third state to join the Union. Trenton, the capital, is now one of the larger cities of this important state.

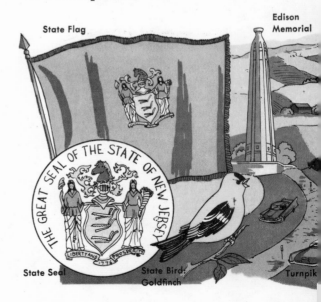

State Flag

Edison Memorial

State Seal

State Bird: Goldfinch

Turnpike

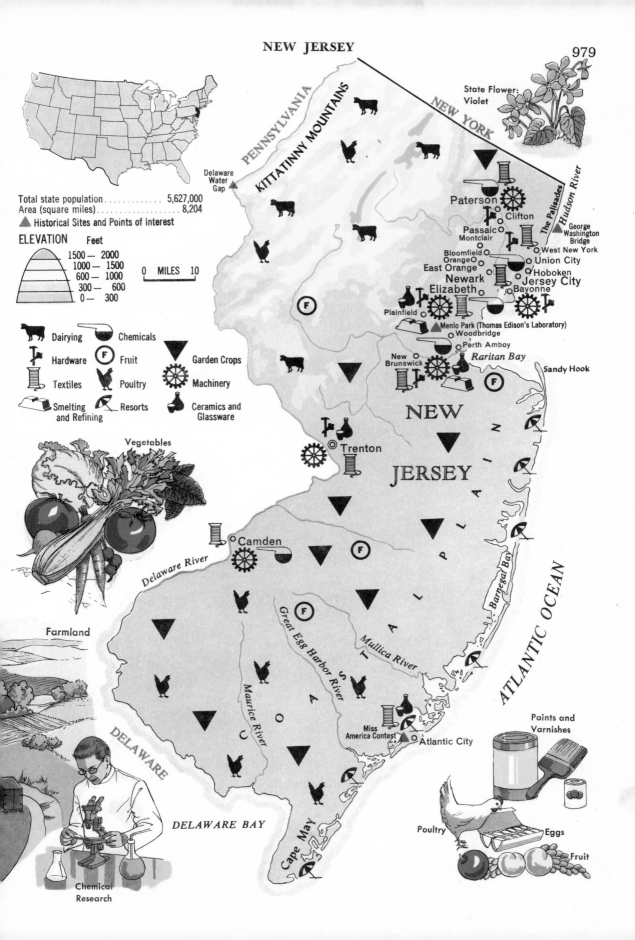

# NEW JERSEY

979

PENNSYLVANIA

KITTATINNY MOUNTAINS

NEW YORK

State Flower:
Violet

Delaware
Water
Gap

Total state population . . . . . . . . . . . . 5,627,000
Area (square miles) . . . . . . . . . . . . . . . 8,204

▲ Historical Sites and Points of Interest

## ELEVATION    Feet

1500 — 2000
1000 — 1500
600 — 1000
300 — 600
0 — 300

0    MILES    10

Paterson

Clifton

The Palisades

Hudson River

Passaic
Montclair

George
Washington
Bridge

Bloomfield
Orange
East Orange

West New York

Union City

Newark

Hoboken

Jersey City

Elizabeth

Bayonne

Plainfield

Menlo Park (Thomas Edison's Laboratory)

Woodbridge

New
Brunswick

Perth Amboy

Raritan Bay

Sandy Hook

### Legend

🐄 Dairying          Chemicals

⚒ Hardware      Ⓕ Fruit

Textiles          🐔 Poultry

Smelting
and Refining     ☂ Resorts

⚙ Garden Crops

⚙ Machinery

Ceramics and
Glassware

Vegetables

NEW

JERSEY

Trenton

ATLANTIC OCEAN

Camden

Delaware River

Great Egg Harbor River

Mullica River

Barnegat Bay

Farmland

Maurice River

Miss
America Contest

Atlantic City

Paints and
Varnishes

DELAWARE

DELAWARE BAY

Cape May

Poultry

Eggs

Fruit

Chemical
Research

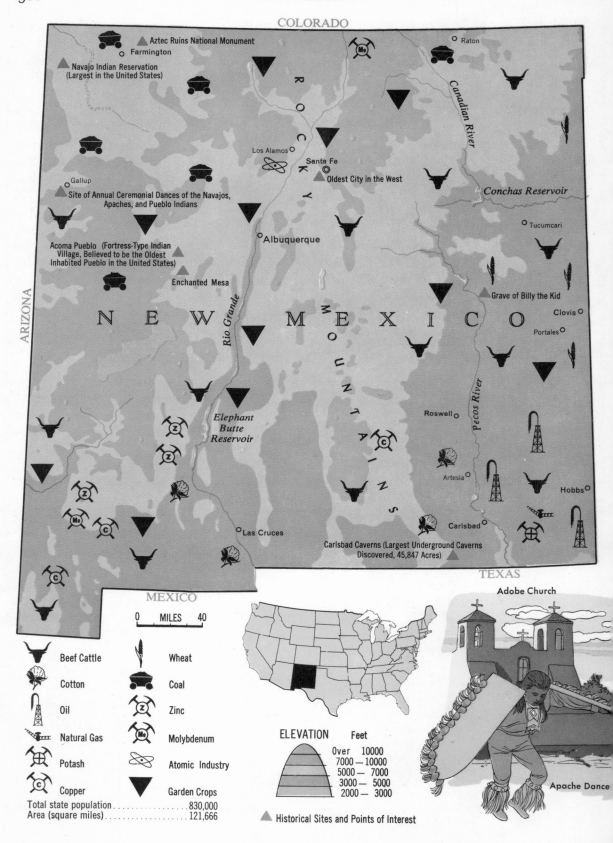

COLORADO

Aztec Ruins National Monument
Farmington
Navajo Indian Reservation
(Largest in the United States)

Mo
Raton

ROCKY

Canadian River

Los Alamos
Santa Fe
Oldest City in the West

Conchas Reservoir

Gallup
Site of Annual Ceremonial Dances of the Navajos,
Apaches, and Pueblo Indians

Tucumcari

Albuquerque

Acoma Pueblo (Fortress-Type Indian
Village, Believed to be the Oldest
Inhabited Pueblo in the United States)

Enchanted Mesa

Grave of Billy the Kid

Clovis

ARIZONA

NEW          MEXICO

Rio Grande

MOUNTAINS

Portales

Elephant
Butte
Reservoir

Z

Z

Z

Roswell

Pecos River

Mo

C

C

Artesia

Hobbs

C

Las Cruces

Carlsbad

Carlsbad Caverns (Largest Underground Caverns
Discovered, 45,847 Acres)

MEXICO

TEXAS

Adobe Church

0     MILES     40

**Legend:**

| Symbol | Label | Symbol | Label |
|---|---|---|---|
| Beef Cattle | | Wheat | |
| Cotton | | Coal | |
| Oil | | Zinc | |
| Natural Gas | | Molybdenum | |
| Potash | | Atomic Industry | |
| Copper | | Garden Crops | |

Total state population..................830,000
Area (square miles)...................121,666

ELEVATION    Feet

Over    10000
7000 — 10000
5000 — 7000
3000 — 5000
2000 — 3000

▲ Historical Sites and Points of Interest

Apache Dance

**NEW MEXICO** This large young state lies in the mountain and tableland country of the Southwest. Only Alaska, Texas, California, and Montana are larger. Only Alaska, Montana, Wyoming, and Nevada are more thinly settled. New Mexico was a province of Spain or Mexico for more than 200 years. Santa Fe was the capital then as it is now. Its Palace of the Governors was built by Spaniards in 1610. In 1848 New Mexico became a part of the United States. In 1912 it became the 47th state in the Union.

New Mexico is called "Land of Enchantment," "Sunshine State," and "Cactus State." Each is a fitting name. Over most of the area rain falls only about 30 days of the year. Under bright-blue skies lie snow-capped and forest-covered mountains and cactus deserts of reddish and yellow soil. The Enchanted Mesa, one of the best-known of the flat-topped lands, and the famous Carlsbad Caverns are in New Mexico. The scenery and the dry, sunny weather attract many vacationers. Many invalids come to health resorts.

Long before white men came to New Mexico, Indians were living there in tall apartment houses built on the faces of rocky cliffs. Other Indians lived in villages called pueblos, in flat-roofed, adobe clay houses. Both the cliff dwellers and the pueblo people irrigated the dry lands near by to grow corn and beans.

The first cattlemen in the New Mexico region were Spaniards. They settled near the Rio Grande River in the late 1500's. They found the land very dry. But they did not give up. They knew how to get along in lands of little rain. They brought cattle, sheep, and horses with them. The Indians there had never seen such animals before.

In 1822 American fur traders came in wagons over the Santa Fe Trail. Soon American settlers followed in stagecoaches to become ranchers and miners.

Today farming is the chief work in New Mexico. Raising livestock is the kind of farming that pays best. Nearly three-fourths of the state is pasture land. Modern irrigation works, such as the Elephant Butte Dam, provide water for some of the land. But only a small portion of the farmland is irrigated. Dry-land farmers raise sorghums, wheat, beans, and chili peppers. Cotton is the state's best money crop on irrigated farms.

Much land in New Mexico is part of large Indian reservations. Most of the Indians are sheepherders.

New Mexico is rich in minerals. Its mines produce petroleum, copper, zinc, coal, gold, silver, and uranium. Factories and mills in the state use some of these mine products. Others are shipped away.

The Indians carry on such industries as making rugs, blankets, silverware, pottery, and paintings. They do their work by hand and sell mainly to tourists.

About half the people of New Mexico live in its cities. The largest cities are Albuquerque, with about 100,000 people, Santa Fe, Roswell, and Carlsbad. New Mexico has become well known through the atomic energy research that has been carried on at Los Alamos.

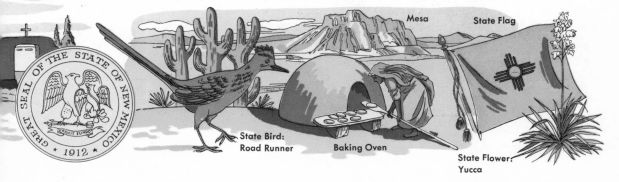

GREAT SEAL OF THE STATE OF NEW MEXICO · 1912 ·

State Bird: Road Runner

Mesa

Baking Oven

State Flag

State Flower: Yucca

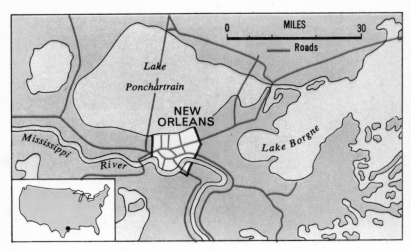

**NEW ORLEANS** Some people say that all American cities look alike. But they are wrong. At least the older parts of many of the older cities in the United States are very different. It is easy to see why they are. The people who founded different cities came from different countries. The buildings they built were like those in the countries they had come from. No other city in the United States looks much like the French quarter—the older part of New Orleans. This city was founded by the French. The houses in the French quarter are famous for their balconies and their beautiful wrought-iron railings.

New Orleans was founded in 1718. Since then it has been under three flags. For more than 40 years the French flag waved over it. Then the French turned it over to Spain. Spain held it for more than 30 years and then gave it back to France. France soon sold it to the United States as a part of the Louisiana Purchase.

New Orleans is on delta land built by the Mississippi River. It is about 100 miles from the mouth of this great river. From the beginning New Orleans was an important port. Ocean vessels could sail up the river to it. River boats could reach it easily. The very first steamboat on the Mississippi was named the "New Orleans."

In early steamboat days the wharves of the city were piled high with bales of cot-

ton. The cotton came from nearby plantations, where it was raised with the help of slaves. An old slave market can still be seen in the French quarter.

Today New Orleans has grown far beyond the French quarter. It is a city of more than half a million people. It is still a leading southern port of the United States. Big ships are tied up to its docks at all times of the year. Some of these ships are fruit boats in from the countries of South America or Central America. New Orleans now has big chemical factories, too.

Tourists visit New Orleans by the thousands every year. During the week before Lent each year the city has a carnival called the Mardi Gras. It is the gayest festival in all the United States. One part of the festival is a great parade down Canal Street, a world-famous street. At Mardi Gras time visitors crowd into the city and fill the hotels. They buy perfume and pralines in the French quarter. They eat at its French restaurants. The tourists help make New Orleans a prosperous city.

The delta land on which the city is built is extremely low. Great levees have been built along the river to keep floods from the city. Getting safe water and getting rid of sewage have been big problems. But the city has solved these problems. It is a pleasant city to live in. (See DELTA; LOUISIANA; MISSISSIPPI RIVER.)

**NEWSPAPERS** There were no newspapers until long after the time of the first books. Newspapers are even much newer than printed books. When Columbus discovered America books were being printed in many cities of Europe, but there were no newspapers. Not until 1609—two years after Captain John Smith and his small band of settlers founded Jamestown—was the first newspaper begun.

"What's the news?" was a common question long before the days of newspapers. In ancient times news was spread from place to place chiefly by travelers. If the news was very important, special messengers might be sent with it. Rulers had their special, royal messengers. "Make way for the messenger of the king," they shouted as they sped along.

In the great days of the Roman Empire newsletters were written and were then copied by slaves and sent to all parts of the Empire. Spoken news thus began to give way to written news. But during the Middle Ages people once more had to depend on "living newspapers." Wandering friars, peddlers, pilgrims, and soldiers of fortune carried ordinary news. Couriers on horseback carried the more important news. In those days, even if newspapers had been published, few except the monks could have read them, for few people could read.

When, late in the Middle Ages, cities were growing to be large and important, town criers came to be the common spreaders of news. A town crier would make his rounds, ringing a bell or blowing a trumpet. As soon as he had a crowd around him, he would tell them the news.

Some of the early printers occasionally printed "broadsides." Broadsides were single sheets of paper with news printed on only one side. Batches of them could be stowed into the packs of peddlers on their way to fairs or other places where there would be crowds of people. These broadsides were not true newspapers for they were not printed regularly.

The first true newspaper was the *Strassburg Relation*. It was a weekly newspaper begun in Strassburg, Germany, in 1609. In 1615 a newspaper was started in Frankfurt and a year later one in Antwerp, in Belgium. Soon there were others. Each of these early newspapers was published by a printer as a part of his regular business. Each printer edited his own paper—that is, he decided what news should appear in the paper and how it should be told.

The first newspapers were much smaller than those we have today. They were really thin news books. The word "newspaper" was not used until 1670.

The early newspapers had to be printed by hand. Besides, there were no good ways of gathering news in those days. It is easy to understand why the papers were small and were weeklies, not dailies.

The first really great newspaper was the daily *Morning Post* of London, which first appeared in 1772. Many famous people wrote for it. Among them were William Wordsworth, Samuel Taylor Coleridge, and Charles Lamb. The *Morning Post* printed news from many countries. More important still, it was the first newspaper to make a point of selling space for advertising. Advertisements filled many of its columns.

**Town criers used to spread the news.**

**THE STORY OF NEWS**

Reporter Gathering Facts

Rewrite Man Getting the Story from a Reporter.

Linotype Operator Setting Type

Close on the heels of the *Morning Post* came the *London Times*. The *Times* quickly became a great newspaper. Many people think that it is still the greatest newspaper in the world.

The story of the newspaper in the United States begins in Boston. In 1690 Benjamin Harris started a monthly newspaper called *Publick Occurrences.* Here is a sample of the news this newspaper had in it:

> While the barbarous Indians were lurking about Chelmsford, there were missing about the beginning of this month a couple of children belonging to a man of that Town, one of them aged about eleven, the other aged about nine years, both of them supposed to be fallen into the hands of the Indians.

*Publick Occurrences* lasted for only one issue. After the first issue, the English governor ordered it stopped.

The first real newspaper of the colonies was the weekly *Boston News-Letter* begun in 1704. At the beginning the foreign news in this newspaper was a year old. But 15 years after it started it was made into a four-page paper and its publisher proudly boasted that his foreign news was less than five months old.

Other newspapers soon followed the *Boston News-Letter.* One of them was pub- lished by James Franklin, the brother of Benjamin Franklin. His friends tried to per- suade James not to start a newspaper. "One newspaper is enough for America," they said. Benjamin helped his brother with this paper. Later Benjamin founded his own newspaper in Philadelphia—the *Penn- sylvania Gazette.*

Publishing a paper in colonial times was not easy. Presses and type were hard to get. Besides, the publishers were always in dan- ger of being put in jail if they printed news which the English rulers did not like.

Not long after the colonies won their freedom several weekly American papers became dailies. To get enough news for a daily paper in those days of no telegraph, telephone, cable, radio, or even railroads, the editors had to work hard. They roamed about to taverns, stores, banks, churches, and wharves for news.

Some editors built schooners to go out to meet incoming boats. Some hired relays of horses to bring news of important events from the nation's capital.

As the amount of news increased, the papers did not add more pages—they sim- ply increased the size of the page. As a re-

Section of the Press in Operation

Conveyor Carrying Completed Papers to the Delivery Room

Newsboy Selling Papers

Truck Making Deliveries

sult, some of the papers were so big that they were called "blanket sheets."

Early in the 19th century the great movement toward the West began. Many printers moved westward along with the other pioneers. In spite of all the hardships, newspapers sprang up in frontier towns.

September 3, 1833, is an important date in the story of the newspaper in America. On that day the first successful cheap newspaper was started. The paper was the *New York Sun*, and it sold for one cent a copy.

When the *Sun* could not get enough exciting news to fill its pages, it "faked" stories. For a week, for example, it ran a series of stories telling about the discovery of life on the moon. The stories fully described the animals and flowers and the "batlike" people of the moon. People believed the stories, and the circulation of the *Sun* jumped to 19,000—the largest circulation of any paper in the world at that time.

In 1835 James Gordon Bennett founded the *New York Herald*. He put many pictures in his paper, and he saw to it that his news was fresh. To get news fast he used homing pigeons. Bennett made himself famous by sending one of his reporters to find the ex-

plorer Livingstone, who was lost in the heart of Africa. The story of how Stanley found Livingstone is very well known. Bennett may have done harm by some of the stories of crime he printed, but he made newspapers popular. Many people who had never read newspapers before became eager to read them.

Among the other famous newspapermen of the 19th century were Horace Greeley and Henry J. Raymond. Greeley, who founded the *New York Tribune*, was a great reformer. One of his fights was against slavery. Raymond, who founded the *New York Times*, adopted as its motto "All the News That's Fit to Print." He made the *Times* an excellent paper. It still is.

Today there are about 1,800 daily papers in the United States. More than 50,000,000 copies of newspapers are sold every day.

The pictures on these two pages show how the news of a local happening gets to the newspaper reader. One such piece of news takes up only a small part of a paper. Every 24 hours each of our great city dailies gathers and prints many tens of thousands of words of reading material. During the week the *New York Times*, for example, prints about 150,000 words a day—enough to fill a good-sized book. In the huge Sunday edition there are about 700,000 words.

We get many kinds of reading material besides the local news for the few cents we pay for a paper. There are news stories from abroad. There are pictures to illustrate the stories. There are editorials in which the editors give their ideas about important questions. There are cartoons and comic strips. There are, too, many columns called features—short stories, articles on health, etiquette, and sports, advice to people who need help, and so on. In addition there are the advertisements. The price we pay for a paper does not begin to cover its cost. Most of the cost of publishing a newspaper is paid by advertisers.

It takes a whole army of workers to put out one of the big daily papers. There are news gatherers, rewrite men, editors, typesetters, make-up men, artists, photographers, printers, and others besides.

Every step in the printing of such a newspaper is a fight against the clock. The time when the paper must be ready for printing is called the deadline. Very shortly after the deadline, the big printing presses begin to roar. The most up-to-date of these presses not only print the papers but also cut them apart, fold them, and even count them. No wonder a newspaper of today is sometimes called a modern miracle.

Fortunately papers do not have to have their own reporters, or news gatherers, scattered all over the world. There are now

Reading the Paper at Home

organizations that gather and sell news to many papers. Many news items are marked AP or UPI. The initials "AP" stand for "Associated Press;" "UPI" for "United Press International." Of course, the telephone, telegraph, cable, and radio have speeded up the gathering of news tremendously. Some of the news in today's papers is less than an hour old. Peary's discovery of the North Pole in 1909 was the first great news story sent to newspapers by radio.

The big presses "eat up" rolls of paper at a tremendous rate. Several miles of paper go through a big press in an hour. One Chicago newspaper tells us that it takes from 30 to 50 acres of spruce trees to make enough paper for it for a single day. The huge Sunday editions of some papers use up thousands of miles of paper!

People do not depend on newspapers for their news as much as they once did. They hear about events on radio and see them on television even sooner than they can read about them in newspapers. But people seem to like to read the news even after they know it from radio and television. **Newspapers, moreover, give their readers more complete information than radio and television usually do. And, as has already been said, readers get much more from newspapers than just the news.** (See ADVERTISING; COMMUNICATION; GREELEY, HORACE; PAPER; PRINTING; RADIO; TELEGRAPH; TELEPHONE.)

**NEWTON, SIR ISAAC** (1642-1727) As a baby Isaac Newton was sickly. During his first few months he was not expected to live. But he grew up to be one of the world's greatest scientists.

All through his boyhood Newton was interested in mechanical toys. He was interested in kites, too. He used to go out early in the morning to fly his kites. Sometimes he tied lighted lanterns to them. Once he frightened the neighbors in this way. They thought they were seeing a comet. Even in

his kite-flying days Newton studied the sky. He often watched the stars, and he made a number of sundials.

Newton stopped school when he was 14. His mother was a widow, and she needed his help on their farm. For the next two years he tried to learn about farming, but he was not very successful. He would begin thinking about some new book or mechanical toy and would forget his work.

His mother finally decided that he would never be a farmer, and sent him to college. In a year or two he began work on the problem that made him famous. The problem was: Why do the planets and moons follow the paths they do? Since they are moving, why do they not go straight out into space?

A story tells that Newton started thinking about gravity when an apple fell from a tree and hit him. The story probably is not true even though gravity does make apples fall from apple trees to the ground.

Before Newton's time, scientists knew something about gravity. They knew that gravity makes objects fall to the ground and keeps houses and people from being hurled off into space. Could it be, Newton asked himself, that the earth pulls the moon and keeps it from running away? And could it be that the sun pulls the earth and the other planets and helps keep them in their paths? Newton thought so.

At first he could not prove that his idea was right. He himself decided that he was on the wrong track. But years later he worked again on the problem and found out that he had been right after all. He then wrote a famous book about gravity.

Newton made many other discoveries. Some of them were about light. He found out, for instance, that sunlight is made up of the rainbow colors. He studied sunlight partly by blowing soap bubbles and watching the colors in them. His neighbors were surprised to see a grown man blowing bubbles for hours at a time.

Newton wanted to find out more about the planets and the other heavenly bodies. But he was not satisfied with the telescopes that were available. To get a better one he invented a new kind—a reflecting telescope. It helped him find out many new things about the sky.

Even after he was famous, Newton was not conceited. Once he said, "If I have seen further than most men, it is by standing on the shoulders of giants." The giants he was thinking of were the great scientists who had lived before his time. (See ASTRONOMY; GRAVITY; LIGHT; PLANETS; SOLAR SYSTEM; TELESCOPE.)

**NEW YEAR'S DAY** The first day of each new year is a holiday in many countries. It is called New Year's Day.

New Year's Day in most places is now January 1. But it has not always been. When George Washington was born, the year began on March 25 in England and America. This was changed in 1752.

Usually there is much merrymaking on New Year's Eve. People like to say goodbye to the old year and welcome to the new one. (See CALENDAR; HOLIDAYS.)

**NEW YORK** This Middle Atlantic state was named for the Duke of York, later James II of England. In 1778 it became the 11th state in the Union. Although only 30th in size, it ranks first in population, first in manufacturing, and first in overseas trade. In it is the largest city in the Americas. Only Tokyo and London have more people than New York City.

Almost nine out of ten people in the state are city dwellers. Most of the cities are in the Hudson-Mohawk Valley and in the New York City area. New York State's farmers live on farms in river valleys or in stretches of gently rolling land.

It is not surprising that people settled where they did. The easiest way across the Appalachians lies in New York State. It follows the Hudson Valley, the Mohawk Valley, and the plain south of Lake Ontario. The route is called the Mohawk Trail.

As population grew, people looked for better ways of travel. Many canals were dug. The most famous was the 350-mile-long Erie Canal along the Mohawk Trail from the Hudson River to Lake Erie. It was a great success from the time it was finished in 1825. Later it was widened and deepened and was named the New York State Barge Canal. Steam and diesel tugs now pull barges along this canal.

Soon after the Erie Canal was completed a railroad was built along the same lowland route. It became part of a main line railroad connecting Chicago and New York City. Later, automobile roads followed the same route. Today it is the route of a new express highway, the New York State Thruway. Airlines follow the Mohawk Trail, too.

The cities along this route are the chief manufacturing cities of the state. The chain of cities begins with New York City, the garment and publishing center, and ends with Buffalo. Albany, the state capital, Troy, and Schenectady are in a group where the Mohawk Valley joins the Hudson lowland. Schenectady is best known

for the manufacture of electrical equipment, and Troy for the shirt and collar industry. Utica, Syracuse, and Rochester are along the canal. Utica is famous for textiles, Syracuse for air-conditioning equipment and chinaware, and Rochester for photographic supplies. Buffalo, a Great Lakes port, has grain elevators, flour mills, and steel plants.

Other things besides their locations have helped manufacturing to grow in these cities. Electricity from power plants at Niagara Falls and on the St. Lawrence, and coal from nearby Pennsylvania mines

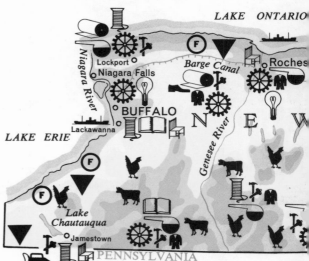

supply power. Forests and stores of natural gas, gypsum, and talc, and products from farms have been useful.

Part of the beauty of New York is in its farmlands. On the rolling or rugged lands of much of the state, most farms are dairy farms. They supply about three-fourths of all the milk needed in the state. There are fine orchards near Lake Ontario and vineyards along the shore of Lake Erie.

Many people enjoy vacationing in the lake and mountain regions of the state. Summers are not hot. Winters, which are cold and snowy, are good for winter sports. Vast numbers visit New York's greatest city. New York City is the key to understanding why New York State is called the Empire State.

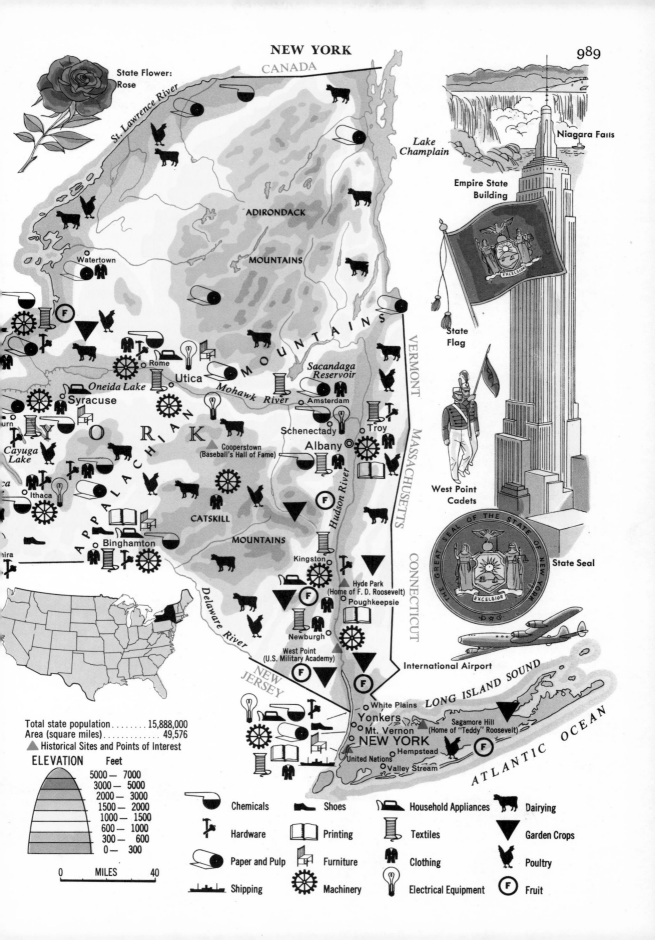

# NEW YORK

State Flower: Rose

CANADA

St. Lawrence River

Lake Champlain

Niagara Falls

ADIRONDACK

MOUNTAINS

Empire State Building

State Flag

Watertown

State Seal

EXCELSIOR

West Point Cadets

Rome

Utica

Mohawk River

Sacandaga Reservoir

Oneida Lake

Syracuse

Amsterdam

Schenectady

Troy

THE GREAT SEAL OF THE STATE OF NEW YORK

Cayuga Lake

Albany

Cooperstown
(Baseball's Hall of Fame)

EXCELSIOR

Ithaca

CATSKILL

Hudson River

Binghamton

MOUNTAINS

Kingston

Hyde Park
(Home of F. D. Roosevelt)

Poughkeepsie

International Airport

Delaware River

Newburgh

West Point
(U.S. Military Academy)

LONG ISLAND SOUND

NEW JERSEY

White Plains

Yonkers

Mt. Vernon

Sagamore Hill
(Home of "Teddy" Roosevelt)

ATLANTIC OCEAN

NEW YORK

Hempstead

United Nations

Valley Stream

Total state population . . . . . . . . 15,888,000
Area (square miles) . . . . . . . . . . . . . 49,576
▲ Historical Sites and Points of Interest

## ELEVATION

| | Feet |
|---|---|
| | 5000 — 7000 |
| | 3000 — 5000 |
| | 2000 — 3000 |
| | 1500 — 2000 |
| | 1000 — 1500 |
| | 600 — 1000 |
| | 300 — 600 |
| | 0 — 300 |

0    MILES    40

Chemicals

Shoes

Household Appliances

Dairying

Hardware

Printing

Textiles

Garden Crops

Paper and Pulp

Furniture

Clothing

Poultry

Shipping

Machinery

Electrical Equipment

F Fruit

VERMONT

MASSACHUSETTS

CONNECTICUT

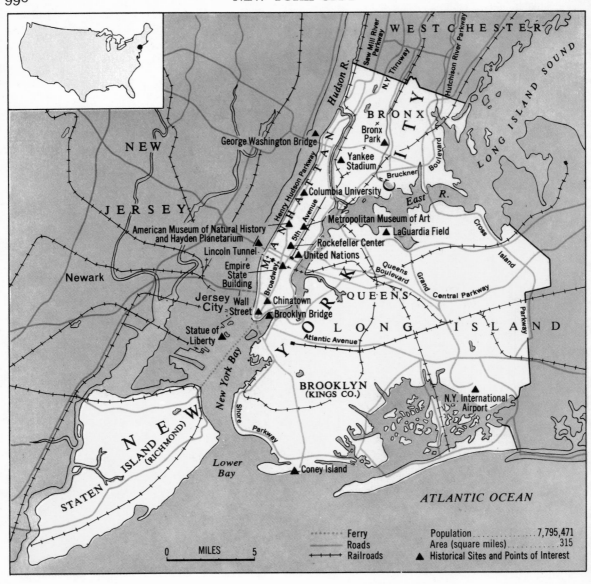

Brooklyn Bridge

Statue of Liberty

New York Skyline

Grand Central Station Information Booth

City Hall

Hansom Cab

**NEW YORK CITY** The words "biggest" and "most" are a great help in telling about New York City. In the whole world only two cities—Tokyo and London—are larger. More than seven million people live in New York City. It has the biggest department store in the United States and the biggest theater. Of all cities it has the most skyscrapers. It has the most miles of subway. It has the most hotels, the most theaters, the most museums, the most concert halls, and the most broadcasting stations. It has the most clothing factories, the most publishing companies, the most banks, and the most visitors. It has the country's busiest railroad station.

The heart of New York is the island of Manhattan. One can take a boat trip all the way around the island. The boat would travel by way of the East River, the Harlem River, and the broad Hudson River. The East and Harlem rivers are not really rivers but straits. The Hudson is a true river and a big one. The world's largest ships steam up it from New York harbor to the city's piers. Cars and trains reach Manhattan by bridge, by tunnel, or by ferryboat.

New York has grown so much that it has spread far beyond the island of Manhattan. There are four other big sections. They are Brooklyn, Queens, Richmond, and the Bronx. Brooklyn and Queens are on Long Island. The largest part of Richmond is on Staten Island. All of the sections of New York City are on islands except the Bronx.

The story of New York begins in 1609. Henry Hudson in that year set up a trading post at the south end of Manhattan Island. A little later the Dutch West India Company built a fort there, and Dutch settlers began to come. In 1626 Peter Minuit, the governor of the colony, bought the whole island from the Indians for 24 dollars' worth of trinkets. The village was named New Amsterdam. In 1664 the British captured it. They changed its name to New York to honor the Duke of York. For a short time in 1673 and 1674 the Dutch held the city again. After that it was in the hands of the British until the end of the Revolution.

Early New York did not look at all like New York today. There were only a few streets. At the north edge of the village a wall was built across the island to protect the settlers from Indians. Wall Street, now the center of the country's banking, follows the line of the old wall. Northward ran Long Highway. This road is now Broadway, famous for its theaters.

In 1789 New York was the capital of the young United States. George Washington was inaugurated president there. But in 1790 Philadelphia was made the capital.

Many things helped the city to prosper. Chief of them was its good harbor. Today New York handles far more ocean shipping than any other port in the United States. There are almost always more than 150 ocean-going vessels at its piers. Some are cargo vessels. Some are big passenger liners. Sea lanes go from New York all over the world. In a year there are more than 12,000 sailings from its piers. Of course, a good harbor is not enough. New York could not have grown so big if goods could not be shipped easily to and from other parts of the country.

There are many thousands of factories in New York. Not many of them make heavy machinery. Instead they make such things as clothing, textiles, leather goods, and electrical equipment.

Visitors in New York find much to see. The world's tallest building—the Empire State Building—is there. So are the United Nations buildings and Rockefeller Center. The Statue of Liberty stands on an island in the harbor. Ocean liners at the piers, art museums, shops, great bridges, places famous in history, plays, operas, concerts, and big sports events—all these help make a visit to New York exciting. (See CITIES; COLONIAL LIFE IN AMERICA; HUDSON, HENRY; LIBERTY, STATUE OF; ROCKEFELLER CENTER; SKYSCRAPERS; UNITED NATIONS.)

**NEW ZEALAND** The beautiful island country of New Zealand is a distant nation in the huge Pacific Ocean. The nearest continent to it, more than 1,200 miles away, is Australia. Like Australia, New Zealand is south of the equator.

Surprising as it may seem, far-off New Zealand is a land of English-speaking people with modern ways of work and play. North Island, South Island, and many other parts in it have English names. Farms and pastures near Christchurch are in a lowland called Canterbury Plains. Mt. Cook is New Zealand's highest mountain and the capital is named Wellington.

Some of the early settlers went to New Zealand because gold was found there. But in Auckland, its largest port, we see signs that today grass, which feeds millions of sheep and cattle, is New Zealand's "gold." Millions of pounds of wool, mutton, and lamb are shipped away. And refrigerated ships carry to other lands so many tons

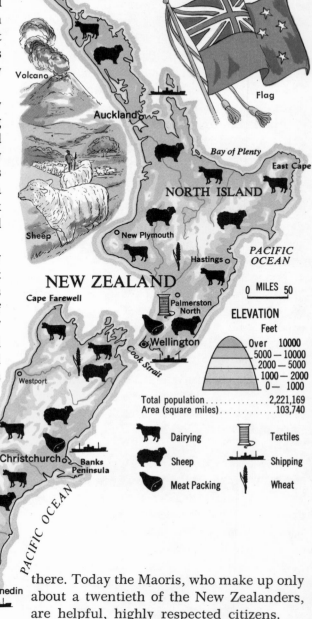

NEW ZEALAND

MILES 0 — 50

ELEVATION
Feet

| Over 10000 |
| 5000 — 10000 |
| 2000 — 5000 |
| 1000 — 2000 |
| 0 — 1000 |

Total population...............2,221,169
Area (square miles)............103,740

Dairying        Textiles

Sheep           Shipping

Meat Packing    Wheat

of butter, condensed milk, and cheese that New Zealand is now one of the world's great dairy countries. Britain is its best customer, and supplies most of New Zealand's imports which include automobiles and oils.

Most English settlements in New Zealand are less than a century old. Early settlers found brown-skinned Maori natives

there. Today the Maoris, who make up only about a twentieth of the New Zealanders, are helpful, highly respected citizens.

New Zealand has some volcanoes and hot springs. December comes in summer there. For Christmas trees, New Zealanders use trees with bright red, real blossoms. But the green pastures, rain, and mild winters and summers help to make people from the British Isles feel at home in New Zealand. Just as Ireland in those islands is called the "emerald isle," New Zealand is a "country of the emerald isles." (See AUSTRALIA; BRITISH EMPIRE.)

**NIAGARA FALLS** The Indians called Niagara Falls "Thunderer of Waters." So much water pours over the falls and down into the gorge below that it does make a noise like thunder. Niagara Falls is one of the great sights of North America.

More than 50 waterfalls in the world are higher than Niagara. Upper Yosemite Falls in California, for instance, is nearly 8 times as high. But not many falls have so much water flowing over them. Not many are so wide. And, although many falls are higher, Niagara Falls is high. It is about 165 feet high—as high as a 16-story building. Niagara Falls is often called the most majestic falls in the world.

Niagara Falls is in the Niagara River. This river carries water from Lake Erie into Lake Ontario. It is on the border between Canada and the United States. Many of the highest waterfalls are in parts of the world that are very hard to reach. Niagara Falls is very easy to reach. Thousands and thousands of people see it every year. Many visit the Cave of the Winds, a cave in the wall of rock back of the falls.

Niagara Falls is divided into two parts. Goat Island is between the two parts. One part is called the American Falls. The other part is called the Horseshoe or Canadian Falls. The American Falls measures 1,000 feet in width. The Horseshoe Falls measures 2,600 feet.

Twenty thousand years ago there was a Niagara Falls. But it was not divided into two parts, and it was not in the same place it is now. In the course of the ages, this great waterfall has gone traveling.

During the great Ice Age much of North America was covered with a vast sheet of ice. For thousands of years the forward edge of the ice was slowly pushed south. Then the weather got warmer and the ice melted back to the north. The same thing happened over and over. Much of the water from the melting ice poured down what is now the valley of the Mississippi. But at last the ice melted back to the north of where the Great Lakes are now. The ice had helped gouge out the basins for these lakes. Water from the melting ice filled them up. It filled them so full that they began to overflow. The water from Lake Erie found a steep cliff in its path. It fell over it, and Niagara Falls was formed.

But the steep cliff was eight miles from where the falls are now. As the water fell over the cliff, it began to wear the edge back. The layer of rock at the top of the cliff was hard limestone. But underneath it there was some softer rock. As the water fell, some of it was hurled backward against this soft rock. It wore away the soft rock. At last the hard upper layer stretched out like a shelf. Then chunks of the "shelf" began to break off. Thus the position of the waterfall slowly changed.

At last the waterfall wore its way back to Goat Island. Then it was divided because part of the river flowed on one side

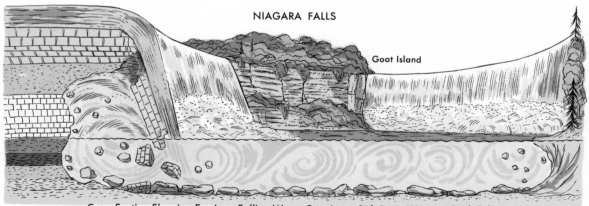

NIAGARA FALLS

Goat Island

Cross Section Showing Erosion—Falling Water Cuts Away Soft Rock, Wearing Back Falls.

of the island and part on the other. In time the falls will wear their way back past Goat Island. Then there will no longer be two separate falls. Still later, scientists think, Niagara Falls will disappear. It will get lower and lower because the layer of hard limestone slopes downward toward Lake Erie. But it has taken thousands of years for the falls to retreat eight miles. It will take thousands more for Niagara Falls to disappear altogether.

Not as much water pours over the falls as poured over 100 years ago. Just above the falls water is now taken from the river and made to fall down through great tubes. It turns water wheels which turn great electric generators. The electric power plants at Niagara are among the biggest in the world. (See EROSION; GREAT LAKES; ICE AGE; WATERFALLS.)

**NICKEL** Pure nickel is a silvery-white metal. It is very hard and tough and strong, and it does not rust easily. It is one of the few metals that magnets attract. Nickel was not discovered until 1751, although for hundreds of years people had used natural mixtures of nickel and other metals found in the earth's crust. Mixtures of metals are called alloys.

Scientists believe that there is a great deal of nickel in the core of the earth. Most of it, unfortunately, is far too deep ever to be reached. And there is not so much nickel in the earth's crust that people can afford to use nickel alone. Instead, it is used to

U.S. Nickel      Bar Magnet      Canadian Nickel

Canadian nickels are magnetic.

coat metals that rust. Or it is mixed with other metals to make alloys. Nickel alloys are as strong and as rust-proof as nickel is by itself.

Nickel-steel, an alloy of nickel and iron, is one of the strongest and toughest kinds of steel made today. It is used for armor plate, engines, bridge beams, and automobile axles. Stainless steel, another alloy of nickel and iron, has chromium added. Magnets made of alnico are far more powerful than any made of ordinary steel. Alnico is an alloy of aluminum, nickel, cobalt, and iron. Invar is another alloy containing nickel and iron. It is used in watch springs and measuring tapes because a strip of it does not change length as the temperature changes.

Monel metal is an alloy of nickel and copper. It is much used for kitchen cabinets, sinks, soda fountains, and cafeteria steam tables. Monel metal can easily be kept bright and shiny. The part of an electric toaster that get red hot is made of still another nickel alloy.

The United States coin we call a nickel does not really contain much of that metal. It is one-fourth nickel and three-fourths copper. It has so little nickel in it that magnets will not attract it. The Canadian nickel contains more nickel, and it is magnetic. During World War II nickel was greatly needed for other purposes than coins. The United States "nickel" then was made from silver, manganese, and copper.

More than three-fourths of all the nickel the world uses comes from mines in Canada. The chief nickel ore is called pentlandite. The picture shows two other ores. (See ALLOYS; IRON AND STEEL; METALS; MINES AND MINING.)

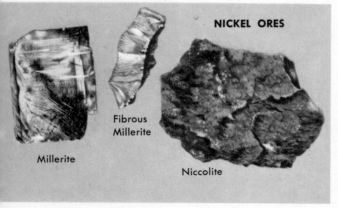

NICKEL ORES

Millerite

Fibrous Millerite

Niccolite

## NIGHTINGALE, FLORENCE (1820-1910)

Many girls today want to be trained nurses. Some of them probably dream of being like Florence Nightingale, a very famous nurse. She was sometimes called the "Angel of the Crimea." Another title for her was "Lady with the Lamp."

Florence Nightingale was English, but she was not born in England. She was born in Florence, Italy. Her father and mother had two homes in England, but they were wealthy and could go traveling about the world whenever they pleased.

When Florence was a girl, most people did not believe in a formal education for young ladies. But Florence did not want to be a young lady of fashion. With her father's help she became well educated. Then she decided that she wanted to study nursing. When she was a little girl she had helped a doctor set a collie's broken leg, and she had been interested in nursing ever since.

In those days most nurses were women with no education. The Nightingales were shocked at the idea of their daughter as a nurse. Nevertheless, Florence went ahead with her plans.

Not long after she became a nurse she decided to go help nurse wounded soldiers. A war had broken out against Russia, and the fighting was going on in the Crimea, a small peninsula in the Black Sea. The English soldiers that were wounded were not being well cared for. She took 38 other nurses with her. Soon they were all hard at work cleaning up the hospitals and seeing that the soldiers had good care and good food. Florence Nightingale, carrying a lamp, often went about during the night to try to make the soldiers more comfortable. She and her helpers kept many soldiers from dying. It can be easily seen why they called her the "Angel of the Crimea" and the "Lady with the Lamp."

While she was in the East she had Crimean fever. She was never strong afterward. She went back to England soon after the war ended, but she did no more nursing. She wrote about nursing, however, and founded a school for nurses that was named after her.

When she was 87 the king of England gave her the Order of Merit for her work. No woman had ever been given this honor before. (See HOSPITALS.)

Florence Nightingale, "The Lady with the Lamp," in a Crimean War Hospital

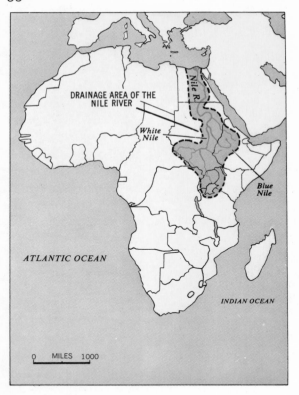

DRAINAGE AREA OF THE NILE RIVER

Nile R.

White Nile

Blue Nile

ATLANTIC OCEAN

INDIAN OCEAN

0    MILES    1000

**NILE RIVER**  The Nile is the longest river in the world. It is 4,000 miles long. The Nile is wide, too. It carries a great deal of water to the Mediterranean Sea.

Most of northern Africa is a vast desert called the Sahara. The Nile flows from south to north across the eastern end of this desert. The valley of the river is an oasis in the desert.

For centuries there was a mystery about the Nile. How could there be such a big river in such a dry land? It took a whole series of explorations from about 1615 to about 1900 to trace the complete length of the Nile. Finally, men found that branches of this important river have their sources in three lakes: Victoria, Albert, and Tana, all in the hot, wet heartland of Africa.

It is no wonder that people were a long time tracing the Nile back to its beginnings. No one can make the trip by boat because there are rapids at several places along the river. These rapids are often called cataracts. Boats cannot pass them. The upper part of the Nile, as the map shows, is called the White Nile. One big branch is called the Blue Nile.

One of the world's oldest civilizations grew up along the Nile. It was ancient Egypt. The river overflowed every year and dropped tons of mud in its valley. The people of Egypt lived on the land the river made rich. There was desert to east and west just as there is now. The Egyptians learned to help the river make the valley an oasis. They took water from the Nile to irrigate their land.

The Egyptians of today still irrigate their land with water from the Nile. But now there are great dams across the river. The dams hold back the water so that the river no longer floods the land. The water stored up back of the dams furnishes a steady supply for irrigation.

The Nile today flows past the pyramids and the ruins of ancient temples. It flows, too, past the city of Cairo, Egypt's capital and one of the world's great cities. Boats sail along the Nile just as they did 5,000 years ago. But now trains travel along its banks, and airplanes fly overhead.

At its mouth the Nile has built one of the biggest deltas in the world. The river divides into several streams as it flows over its delta. It built the delta out of mud that it carried. Some of the mud may have traveled 2,000 miles. (See CANALS; DELTA; EGYPT; IRRIGATION; LAKES; PYRAMIDS; RIVERS; SUEZ CANAL.)

**NITROGEN**  Almost four-fifths of the air is made up of the gas nitrogen. Nitrogen, like all the gases in the air, is invisible.

Our bodies have to have nitrogen, but we cannot use the nitrogen from the air. We breathe it in and then breathe it right out again. We get the nitrogen we need from the food we eat. Milk, meat, eggs, and cheese have nitrogen in them.

This gas is one of the substances called elements, the building blocks of all the other substances. But nitrogen is not a very good "joiner." It is often called a lazy gas.

Even when it does join some of the other elements it sometimes acts as if it did not want to stay joined. Many of our explosives have nitrogen in them. When the nitrogen breaks away they explode.

All living material is part nitrogen. We ourselves, therefore, are part nitrogen. If some of the food we eat did not have nitrogen in it, we could not grow or replace the worn-out cells in our bodies.

Nitrogen is such a poor joiner that we might not get enough food with nitrogen in it if it were not for the tiny plants called bacteria. Some bacteria take nitrogen from the air and join it to other materials in the soil. Then larger plants can get nitrogen from the soil. And we can get nitrogen by eating certain parts of these plants or by eating animals that eat the plants.

Even though we cannot use the nitrogen from the air, it makes the air better to breathe. The nitrogen weakens the oxygen —the part of the air we have to have. Oxygen mixed with nitrogen is much better for us than pure oxygen would be. (See AIR; BACTERIA; CROP ROTATION; ELEMENTS; EXPLOSIVES; FIREWORKS; FOODS; LEGUMES.)

NOAH AND THE FLOOD

**NOAH'S ARK**  God, a Bible story says, told Noah that there would be a great flood. He told him to build a big boat, or ark, and to put on it a pair of every kind of animal on earth. Noah built the ark. He and his family and all the animals went aboard and lived on the ark during the flood.

After the rains had stopped, Noah sent a dove away from the ark. The dove brought back an olive twig. Then Noah knew that some trees were no longer covered with water. Soon the ark came to rest on a mountain. (See BIBLE; BIBLE STORIES.)

Lumps on clover roots contain bacteria which take nitrogen from the air and add it to the soil.

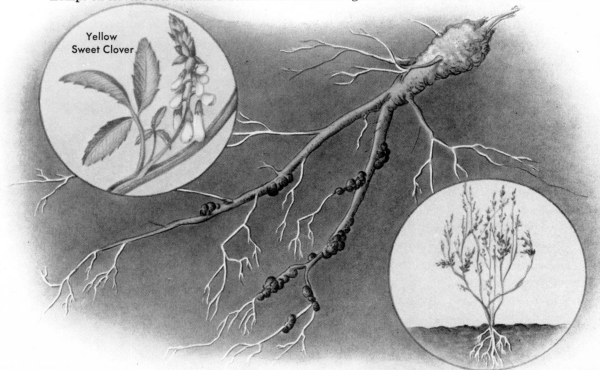

Yellow
Sweet Clover

**NOMADS** Nomads are wandering herdsmen. They have no year-round homes. They do not plant any crops. Instead they move from place to place to find food for their flocks and herds.

There was a time when our ancestors had no domesticated animals and no cultivated plants. They had to get all their food from wild plants and animals. If the animals they hunted moved to find new pasture, these people followed them. Nomads today live much as our ancestors did thousands of years ago. But modern nomads have flocks and herds of tame animals.

Nomads do not live an easy life. As a rule they live in tents. They have almost no furniture. Furniture is too hard to carry from place to place. Their beds and chairs are rugs or skins spread on the ground. For cooking and eating, nomads have a few pots and bowls. They own few clothes besides those that they wear every day.

The nomads of today live chiefly in the deserts and the almost-desert regions of the world. There are nomads in the Sahara in Africa. There are also nomads in Arabia and in the desert regions farther to the east in Asia. Not all nomads live in hot regions. Some of the Lapps are nomads. So are some of the Eskimos. In the hot deserts the nomads own sheep, goats,

Eskimos use huskies to pull their sleds over the ice.

horses, and camels. Those who live in the Far North have herds of reindeer instead.

Most of the time the nomads get along peacefully with the people of the farms and villages they come near. In the Sahara, for instance, the nomads come to the villages in the oases. They trade sheep, goats, camels, wood, and leather to the villagers for dates, vegetables, and grain.

But there have been times when nomads were not able to find food for their animals. Then they have been driven to rob farms and villages. Long ago the people of China built the Great Wall of China to protect themselves from the tribes of nomads in the dry lands to the northwest. This wall was about 1,500 miles long. More than once hordes of nomads have come into eastern Europe from Asia. Many of these nomads stayed to become farmers.

In some parts of the world where there were once only tribes of nomads there is now fertile farm land and industry. But in the more barren parts of the world there will probably always be nomads. (See ESKIMOS; GYPSIES; LAPLAND; MONGOLIA; SAHARA.)

Desert nomads wander from place to place seeking new grazing grounds for their animals. Their tent homes pack up easily and are light enough to be carried with them each time they move.

**NORSE GODS AND GODDESSES** The Vikings, or Norsemen, believed in many gods and goddesses. Almost everything that happened, these people thought, was the work of a god or goddess. In a thunderstorm they said, "Thor is driving his chariot and hurling thunderbolts." When spring came, they said, "Iduna is waking up after her long sleep." When a dry spell spoiled their crops, they said, "Loki has played one of his pranks." Thor was the god of thunder, Iduna the goddess of spring, and Loki the mischief-maker.

The gods and goddesses of the Norsemen were very much like ordinary people. They had the same faults that people have. And they died, too, just as people do. The Norsemen loved some of their gods and goddesses. They were afraid of others.

The names for some of the Norse gods and goddesses are hidden in our names for some of the days of the week. Tuesday is "Tiu's day." Tiu was the god of war. Wednesday is "Woden's day." Woden was the chief god. Thursday is "Thor's day." Friday is "Frigg's day." Frigg was the wife of Woden and the goddess of the sky.

Among the other gods and goddesses were Balder and his twin brother Hoth; Frey and his sister Freya, and Niord. Balder was the god of light, and Hoth the god of darkness. Frey was the god of sunlight and showers, and Freya the goddess of beauty. Niord was the god of the sea.

Their gods and goddesses, the Norsemen believed, lived in Asgard, a wonderful place above the clouds. Valhalla was a great hall for heroes killed in battle. The rainbow was a bridge to Asgard.

The Norsemen made up many stories about their gods and goddesses. These stories explained many of the happenings around them that they could not understand. They satisfied their wonder about lightning by saying that Thor was hurling a weapon about. Stories of this kind are called myths. (See DAYS OF THE WEEK; MYTHS AND LEGENDS; VIKINGS.)

NORSE GODS

Woden

Hoth

Thor

Frey

Niord

**NORTH AMERICA** The third largest of the seven continents in size is North America. Only Asia and Africa are larger. It is third largest in population, too. Only Asia and Europe have more people.

All of North America is north of the equator. But the southernmost part of North America is so far south that it is very warm all the year round. The northernmost part of the continent goes beyond the Arctic Circle into the region of very long, very cold winters. Somewhere in this big continent it is possible to find almost any kind of climate one could want—hot or cold, wet or dry, a climate that changes greatly with the seasons or one that is much the same all the year round.

It is possible to find almost any kind of scenery one could want, too. There are snow-capped mountains and great nearly-flat plains. There are rocky coasts and sandy beaches. There are deserts and swamps. There are lakes of many shapes and sizes. There are glaciers and waterfalls and smoking volcanoes. Of course, there are thousands of towns and cities.

North America has some of the most wonderful sights in the world. Its forests of coast redwoods and big trees are among them. Among them, too, are the geysers and hot springs of Yellowstone Park, the Grand Canyon of the Colorado River, and Niagara Falls. Huge dams and reservoirs, sky-

GREENLAND

HUDSON

BAY

CANADA

GREAT LAKES

Montreal

Ottawa

St. Lawrence R.

Detroit

Chicago

Cleveland

New York

Philadelphia

Washington, D.C.

APPALACHIAN MTS.

Ohio R.

AMERICA

St. Louis

Missouri R.

Mississippi R.

New Orleans

ATLANTIC OCEAN

GULF OF MEXICO

ARCTIC OCEAN

GREENLAND (DEN.)

ALASKA

Baffin Bay

Hudson Bay

CANADA

PACIFIC OCEAN

UNITED STATES

ATLANTIC OCEAN

MEXICO

GULF OF MEXICO

CUBA

PUERTO RICO

DOM. REP.

HAITI

BR. HOND.

HONDURAS

GUATEMALA

EL SALVADOR

NICARAGUA

COSTA RICA

PANAMA

0 MILES 1000

0 MILES 1000

## NATURAL VEGETATION

- Ice Cap
- Grasslands
- Tundra or Heath
- Bushes and Shrubs
- Desert Vegetation
- Broadleaf Evergreen Trees
- Broadleaf Shedding Trees
- Needleleaf Evergreen Trees
- Mixed Evergreen and Shedding Trees

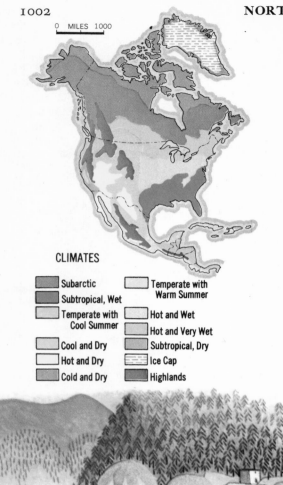

0   MILES   1000

**CLIMATES**

| | |
|---|---|
| Subarctic | Temperate with Warm Summer |
| Subtropical, Wet | |
| Temperate with Cool Summer | Hot and Wet |
| | Hot and Very Wet |
| Cool and Dry | Subtropical, Dry |
| Hot and Dry | Ice Cap |
| Cold and Dry | Highlands |

In Alaska, steep mountains rise up from the sea.

New York City is a busy eastern port.

scrapers, bridges, monuments, and ancient pyramids and pueblos are some of its man-made wonders.

The continent has riches of many kinds. Millions of acres of fertile soil make up its fine farmlands. It has great stores of coal, petroleum, copper, and iron. It has smaller stores of many other valuable minerals such as uranium and nickel. Its big rivers provide vast amounts of water power. Its Great Lakes are a wonderful waterway.

North America is divided among nine countries. But, as the maps show, some of them have a much bigger share of it than others. The biggest country is Canada. It is bigger than the 50 states of the United States. The United States comes after Canada. Then comes Mexico. Mexico, although it is much smaller than either Canada or the United States, is a big country. It is almost exactly the size of Britain, France, Germany, Spain, and Italy put together. The other six countries are south of Mexico. They are in the part of North America that is called Central America. All six of these countries are small. In Central America there is also a tiny British colony, British Honduras.

Since North America has riches of many kinds, it is not surprising that its people earn their livings in many different ways. Some of them live very simply. The Eskimos, for instance, do. Others—many, many of them—live in the hurry and noise of big cities. There are 16 cities with over a million people each. A great many city people work in factories.

Of course, in this big continent with all its different climates, there are wild plants and animals of many kinds. Orchids and reindeer moss, polar bears and monkeys, cactus plants and cattails, prairie grass and tree ferns, rattlesnakes and whitefish—all can be found in North America.

**Citrus fruits are raised in warm areas.**

Open pit mining is carried on near the Great Lakes.

The harbors on the Great Lakes are shipping points for the copper, iron ore, and grain of the region.

For many centuries the only people in North America were Indians. After Columbus found the New World, other explorers soon followed. Because of its great riches people from many lands began flocking to it. Most of them came from countries in Europe. A few came from Asia and Africa. Although North America's population has grown fast, the continent is still not nearly as crowded as Europe. There is still room for the population of North America to grow. (See CANADA; CENTRAL AMERICA; MEXICO; UNITED STATES.)

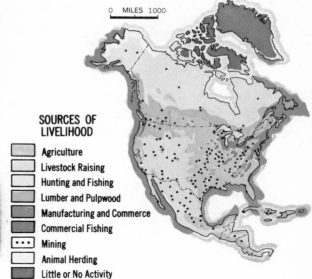

0 MILES 1000

**SOURCES OF LIVELIHOOD**

- Agriculture
- Livestock Raising
- Hunting and Fishing
- Lumber and Pulpwood
- Manufacturing and Commerce
- Commercial Fishing
- Mining
- Animal Herding
- Little or No Activity

Huge steel mills change the iron into steel.

In the stockyards, buyers examine the cattle.

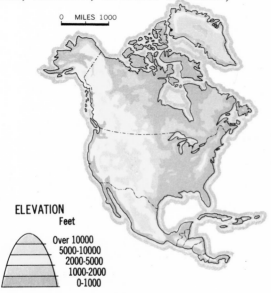

0 MILES 1000

**ELEVATION**
Feet

Over 10000
5000-10000
2000-5000
1000-2000
0-1000

Huge dams help turn water power into electricity.

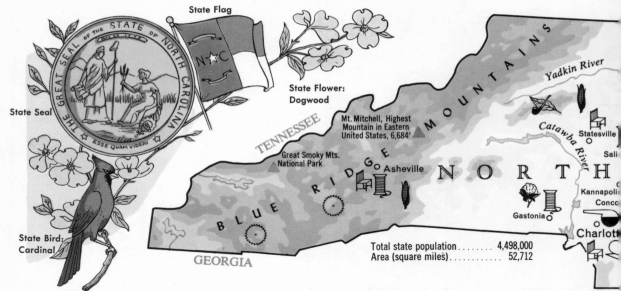

State Flag

State Seal

State Flower: Dogwood

State Bird: Cardinal

TENNESSEE

Mt. Mitchell, Highest Mountain in Eastern United States, 6,684'

Great Smoky Mts. National Park

BLUE RIDGE MOUNTAINS

Asheville

Yadkin River

Catawba River

Statesville

Sali

Kannapoli

Conco

Gastonia

Charlott

N O R T H

GEORGIA

Total state population . . . . . . . 4,498,000
Area (square miles) . . . . . . . . . . . 52,712

## NORTH CAROLINA

**NORTH CAROLINA** The state of North Carolina is in southeastern United States. The first settlers came to the region between 1585 and 1587. They were given aid for their journey by Sir Walter Raleigh. Their homes on Roanoke Island made up the first English settlement in North America. There, in 1587, the first English-American child, Virginia Dare, was born. But the Roanoke settlement soon mysteriously disappeared. It is called the "Lost Colony."

The first permanent settlement was made in the region about 1650. In 1663 King Charles II granted "Charles Land" or "Carolina" to eight lords. The colony did not prosper, partly because of poor governing by the owners. In 1729 Carolina was divided into North Carolina and South Carolina. North Carolina was the first of the 13 colonies to vote for independence from England. In 1789 it became the 12th state of the Union. Its capital is Raleigh.

North Carolina ranks as a middle-sized state in area, but it is tenth in population. It has more people than any of the other southeastern states. Two out of three of its people live on farms or in small villages. Only one city, Charlotte, has a population of over 100,000.

The farms of the state look much better today than they did for many years. Soils which had been worn out have been made to produce good crops again. Farm homes are in good repair. Most of North Carolina's farm homes have electricity.

Some cotton is raised. But the big money crop is tobacco. The best tobacco is grown on the warm coastal plain and in the Piedmont region—the plateau between the coastal plain and the mountains. North Carolina farmers produce more tobacco than is produced in any other state. Some farmers are turning to dairy farming.

The Piedmont is the manufacturing region. Almost 75 years ago men developed electric power at falls in the many mountain streams. Cotton mills were the first to use this electric power. Today there are hundreds of factories that use it. Cotton and other textile mills rank first among them. Some of the newer textile mills make rayon, nylon, and Dacron. Charlotte is the center of the textile industry. Clustered around the city are many small mill towns, each with its textile mill and rows of workers' homes. Many workers, however, live on farms and drive to the textile mills.

Furniture and paper factories make use of wood from the state's forests. Tobacco manufacturing gives work to many. The world's largest cigarette factories are at Winston-Salem, Reidsville, and Durham.

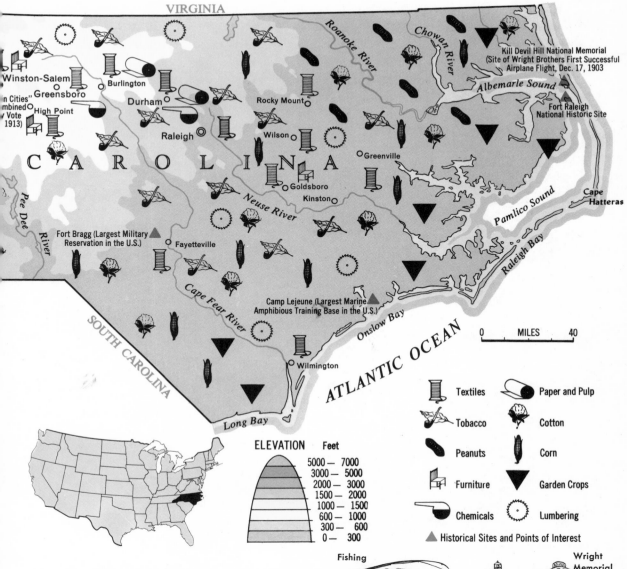

VIRGINIA

Winston-Salem
Greensboro
Burlington
Durham
High Point
"n Cities" mbined Vote 1913)

Rocky Mount
Raleigh
Wilson
Goldsboro
Kinston

Greenville

C A R O L I N A

Roanoke River
Chowan River
Albemarle Sound
Kill Devil Hill National Memorial (Site of Wright Brothers First Successful Airplane Flight, Dec. 17, 1903
Fort Raleigh National Historic Site

Pee Dee River

Neuse River

Fort Bragg (Largest Military Reservation in the U.S.)
Fayetteville

Cape Fear River

Camp Lejeune (Largest Marine Amphibious Training Base in the U.S.)

Onslow Bay

Wilmington

SOUTH CAROLINA

Long Bay

Pamlico Sound
Cape Hatteras
Raleigh Bay

ATLANTIC OCEAN

MILES 0 — 40

## ELEVATION    Feet

| Elevation | Feet |
| --- | --- |
| 5000 — 7000 | |
| 3000 — 5000 | |
| 2000 — 3000 | |
| 1500 — 2000 | |
| 1000 — 1500 | |
| 600 — 1000 | |
| 300 — 600 | |
| 0 — 300 | |

Textiles    Paper and Pulp
Tobacco    Cotton
Peanuts    Corn
Furniture    Garden Crops
Chemicals    Lumbering
Historical Sites and Points of Interest

North Carolina has good roads over which many visitors travel each year. Great Smoky Mountains National Park is especially lovely in late spring when rhododendrons are in bloom. Very different is the scenery along the new highway on the sandy reef leading to beyond Cape Hatteras. Here lighthouses, both old and new, warn ships of the dangers along the coast. Some of the people in the small fishing villages on the long reef do not like to think of the changes the new highway may bring. They have been happy with their simple ways of living.

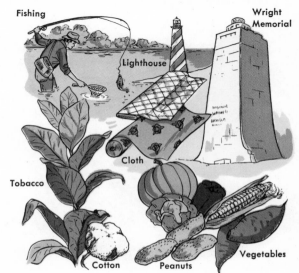

Fishing
Wright Memorial
Lighthouse
Cloth
Tobacco
Cotton
Peanuts
Vegetables

**NORTH DAKOTA** This central state was the northern part of the Dakota Territory. The territory got its name from the Dakota Indians who lived there before it was opened for homesteaders in 1863. Later, when the territory was made into two states, both states wanted the name Dakota. The matter was settled by naming them North Dakota and South Dakota. The two Dakotas became states in 1889.

Frenchmen from Canada had explored this region in the 1700's. Fur-trading posts were built as early as 1797. The first attempt for a permanent settlement was made at Pembina in 1812. But settlement in the Dakota country was slow, in part because of Indian attacks.

The coming of the railroads in the 1870's and the invention of modern farm machines hastened settlement. Among American and European pioneers, the largest group came from Norway. They were a hardy, brave people. They were not afraid of the long cold winters and the summers, often too hot and dry. To them it was a land of opportunity. Timber was scarce both in the tall-grass prairies in the eastern half and on the short-grass Great Plains in the western half. Many settlers built sod houses for their first homes. The pioneers' big money crop was wheat. Every village had its row of grain elevators beside the railroad tracks. Long trains carried the grain to cities farther east.

Today, in spite of blizzards, floods, dry years, dust storms, grasshoppers, and plant diseases, North Dakota produces more wheat than any other state except Kansas. In hard spring wheat and in durum wheat, from which macaroni is made, it ranks first in the United States. The farmers, however, no longer depend on wheat alone. In the fertile Red River Valley and on the prairies, farmers have dairy cows and poultry. They also fatten livestock. Flax and sugar beets are important crops. On the plains, much livestock is raised. Some wheat is grown by dry farming.

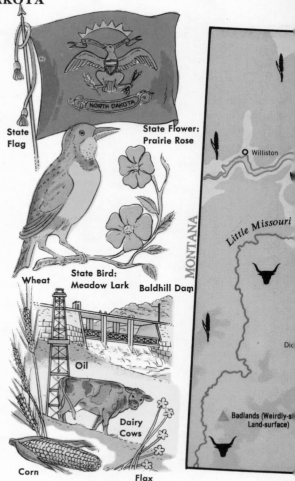

State Flag

State Flower: Prairie Rose

State Bird: Meadow Lark

Wheat

Oil

Dairy Cows

Corn

Flax

Baldhill Dam

MONTANA

Williston

Little Missouri

Badlands (Weirdly-s Land-surface)

Farmers have special machines that grind the soil to make a deep powder-like blanket. This holds the moisture and gives the next year's crop a good start. Water for irrigating some land is supplied by the Garrison Dam on the Missouri River, and several other dams.

North Dakota is one of the larger states. It is still only thinly settled. About three-fourths of the people live on farms or in very small towns. Farms range from about 160 acres to several thousand acres. Farming is the main interest of the people and good farmland the greatest of their riches. However, there are some riches under the grasslands. Lignite or brown coal is mined with steam shovels. The coal is made into bricks that burn very much like charcoal. Oil is being pumped from a new strike at Tioga, near Williston.

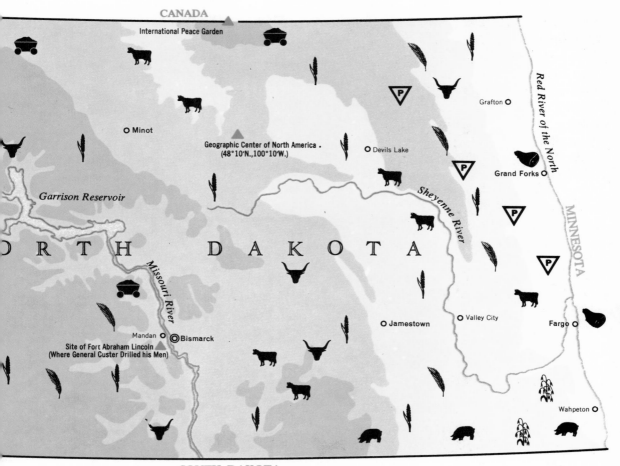

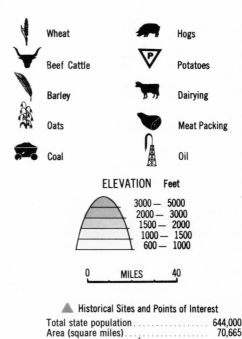

The capitol at Bismarck towers above the fields where whirring combines may be harvesting wheat. The cabin in which Theodore Roosevelt lived as a young man has been moved to the grounds of the capitol. He came to North Dakota's "wild west" to raise cattle.

Fargo, although it has only about 40,000 people, is North Dakota's largest city. It is the trade and manufacturing center for this vast farming region. With their millions of acres of crop land, North Dakota people look forward to a bright future.

Wheat
Hogs

Beef Cattle
Potatoes

Barley
Dairying

Oats
Meat Packing

Coal
Oil

ELEVATION Feet

3000 — 5000
2000 — 3000
1500 — 2000
1000 — 1500
600 — 1000

0 MILES 40

▲ Historical Sites and Points of Interest

Total state population.................. 644,000
Area (square miles)...................  70,665

**NORTH POLE** At one place on the earth it is impossible to go north. That place is the North Pole. "North" means "toward the North Pole," and at the North Pole it is impossible to go any farther north. At the North Pole no one could go east or west, either. The only possible direction to go would be south.

The earth spins on its axis like a top as it travels around the sun. The North Pole is at one end of this axis. At the other end is the South Pole.

There is ice and snow at the North Pole all the year long. And for almost half the year no sunshine reaches it. For the rest of the year, however, it is light all the time. At the North Pole, then, the sun rises and sets only once a year.

The first person to reach the North Pole was Robert E. Peary. He reached it in 1909. (See EARTH; PEARY, ROBERT E.)

**NORTH SEA** The North Sea is just east of Great Britain. Norway, Denmark, Germany, the Netherlands, Belgium, and France also have coasts along this sea.

The North Sea is only a few hundred feet deep. The shallowness of the water helps make this sea a good place for fish of many kinds. Three-fourths of all the fish sold in England are caught there. Fishing boats from all the countries that border the North Sea dot its waters.

No sea in the world is busier. Many, many ships go back and forth across it. The busiest ocean routes of the world come together there. The great Rhine River, which is itself a busy highway, flows into it. So do the Elbe, the Thames, and several other important rivers. On or near its shores are some of the world's greatest ports. London, Hamburg, and Rotterdam are three of them. (See FISHING; SHIPS.)

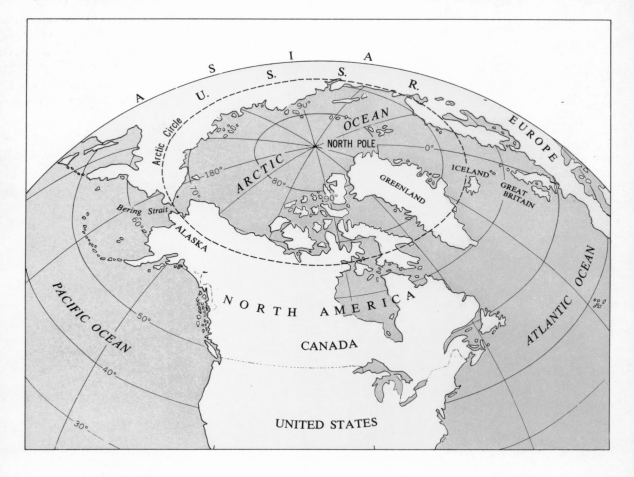

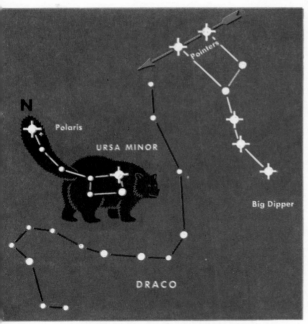

The North Star is often called Polaris.

**NORTH STAR** Most stars rise and set or seem to move in a big circle in the sky. But there is one star that is in almost exactly the same place in the sky all night long and every night. It is the North Star. The spinning of the earth makes the other stars appear to move. The North Star does not move from its place because the earth's axis is pointed toward it. It is almost exactly above the North Pole.

The North Star is in the group of stars that is called the Little Dipper. It is the last star in the handle of the dipper. Two stars in the Big Dipper are a help in finding the North Star. They are called the Pointers. An imaginary line drawn through them points to the North Star.

There are many stars brighter than the North Star. But none is more important. In the northern half of the world the North Star has guided people on their travels for many centuries by helping them tell their directions. South of the equator it cannot serve as a guide because it cannot be seen.

Besides telling directions from the North Star, a person can tell from it how far north of the equator he is. The farther one goes north, the higher the North Star

is in the northern sky. Just north of the equator the North Star is just above the northern horizon. In a place halfway between the equator and the North Pole, the North Star is halfway between the northern horizon and the "top of the sky" — the zenith. At the North Pole itself the star is almost exactly at the zenith.

The North Star is often called the pole-star. Another name for it is Polaris.

Polaris has not always been the North Star, nor will it always be. The earth's axis little by little changes its direction. Several thousand years ago the star Thuban was the North Star. In some 12,000 years our North Star will be the bright-blue star Vega. (See ASTRONOMY; COMPASS; SKY; STARS; ZENITH.)

The pointers in the Big Dipper help locate Polaris.

**NORWAY** Each summer hundreds of tourists go to northern Norway to see the midnight sun. The tip of Cape Nordkyn on Norway's northern coast is farther north than any other place in the mainland of Europe. In Norway's "Far North," visitors also like to see Lapp reindeer herders. And most tourists want to travel along Norway's very long west coast. Long, high mountain ranges run north and south near that coast. Deep, narrow arms of the sea reach far into the mountains. They are called fiords. Taking care of visitors helps many Norwegians to earn a living.

A thousand years ago Norwegian Vikings were already making daring sea voyages. Today, too, many Norwegians sail the seas. Some are fishermen. Big catches of fish are made near Norway. Other Norwegians catch whales near far-off Antarctica. Many of Norway's men of the sea work on big ocean freighters. Some freighters sail between Norway and other lands. But others do not visit home ports often. They are hired by foreign countries to carry goods between various foreign ports, and are busy sailing the Atlantic, the Pacific, and the Indian Ocean. Norway is one of the world's great "carrying nations."

Bergen is the biggest city on Norway's western coast. Ocean freighters and liners, smaller coastal steamers, and fishing boats come and go from its deep harbor. Trains, busses, and airplanes link the city with other places in Norway. Among Bergen's many factories are those for canning fish and making fish products.

The west coast harbors do not freeze over, for winds from the Atlantic bring some winter warmth. On many tiny bits of lowland, potatoes, oats, and hay are raised. They are crops that are able to grow where summers are short, cool, and rainy. Farmers sell milk and cheese. They keep cows in high pastures in summer. In wintertime the cows are kept in barns and fed oats and hay. Sometimes farmers store topsoil in cellars to keep winter winds from blowing it away. In spring they spread it on their tiny fields again.

There is more lowland near Trondheim than at any other place along the western coast. In early times that seaport was Norway's capital. Even today Norway's kings and queens must be crowned in Trondheim's beautiful Nidaros Cathedral.

The king's palace and Norway's government buildings are now in Oslo, the country's capital and biggest city. Oslo is famous, too, for its harbor, its university, and its parks. And many kinds of beautiful things made by Norwegians are to be seen in its museums and shops. The city is in the southeastern part of Norway.

More than half of Norway's people live in the southeastern lowlands. In these lowlands there is room for large farms. There is more sunshine and less rain than in the west. Farmers grow wheat to sell. Much of Norway's forest land is in the southeast. Logs for pulp and paper mills are cut from its forests. Products of those mills, together with fish and fish products, are Norway's chief exports.

Norway is poor in coal but rich in water power used in making electricity for its many factories. And both its city and farm homes have long had electricity. Fish, forests, fiords, and waterfalls are important riches. (See DAY AND NIGHT; DENMARK; FIORD; SWEDEN; VIKINGS.)

Puffin

Nidaros Cathedral

Wheat

Potatoes     Dairying

Sheep

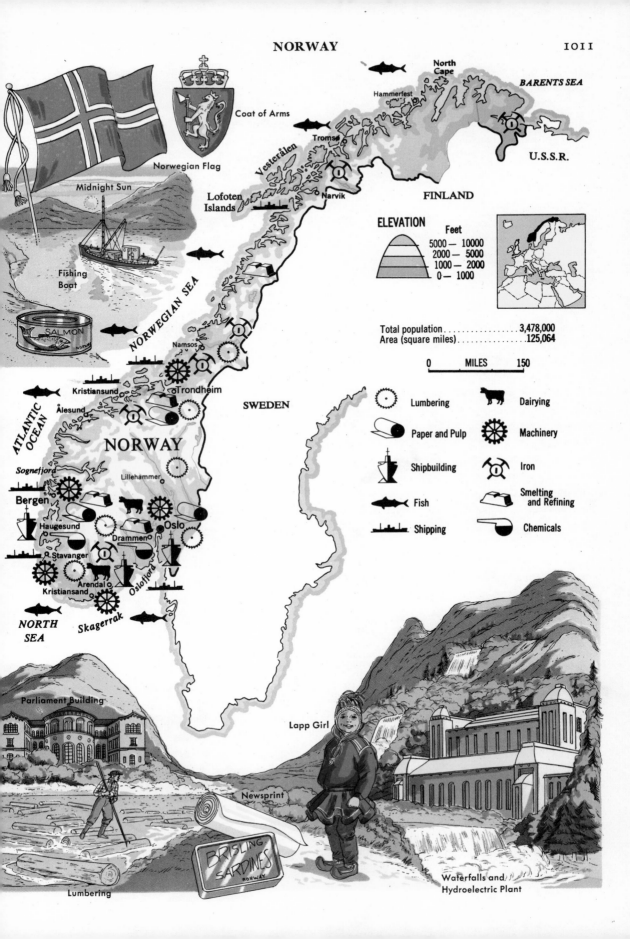

Coat of Arms

Norwegian Flag

Midnight Sun

Fishing Boat

SALMON

*NORWEGIAN SEA*

North Cape

*BARENTS SEA*

Hammerfest

Tromsø

Vesterålen

Narvik

FINLAND

U.S.S.R.

Lofoten Islands

**ELEVATION**

Feet
5000 — 10000
2000 — 5000
1000 — 2000
0 — 1000

Total population . . . . . . . . . . . . . . . 3,478,000
Area (square miles) . . . . . . . . . . . . . . 125,064

0        MILES        150

Namsos

Trondheim

Kristiansund

Ålesund

*ATLANTIC OCEAN*

**NORWAY**

SWEDEN

*Sognefjord*

Lillehammer

Bergen

Haugesund

Drammen

Oslo

Stavanger

Oslofjord

Arendal

Kristiansand

*NORTH SEA*

*Skagerrak*

Lumbering

Paper and Pulp

Shipbuilding

Fish

Shipping

Dairying

Machinery

Iron

Smelting and Refining

Chemicals

Parliament Building

Lapp Girl

Newsprint

BRISLING SARDINES
NORWAY

Lumbering

Waterfalls and Hydroelectric Plant

Cave man used stones to tell of animals he had seen.

**NUMBERS** By the time they start to school most children can count, at least up to four or five. No one thinks anything of it. Counting seems easy. But it took our early ancestors a long, long time to learn to count. Not so very many thousands of years ago no one could count at all.

Early shepherds named their sheep. When they wanted to know whether all the sheep were there, they said over the names. It was like calling the roll in a class instead of counting to see that everyone is present. People kept track of other things, too, by giving them names.

When people first began to count they did not use number names like "one," "two," and "three." They used counters instead. Sometimes they used pebbles. Even today an Apache Indian keeps track of his ponies by carrying in a leather pouch a pebble to stand for each pony. The ancient Chinese used short sticks as counters. Some Indian tribes used shells.

But the counters used most often were the fingers. Ten is a very important number in our system of numbers. We count by tens and tens of tens. Ten came to be such an important number because a person has ten fingers.

Counting by using number names is much more convenient than counting with sticks or shells or pebbles. Sometimes there are no sticks or shells or pebbles near by. Number names, which a person carries in his head, are always ready to use. Fingers are always ready to use, too. But for num-

bers above ten, number names are easier to use than fingers. It would be easy to show how many days there are in a week by holding up seven fingers. But how hard it would be to show how many days there are in a whole year!

Although number names are a big help, making up a whole set of number names is not an easy task. There are still tribes that have no names for numbers above three or four. For numbers that are bigger they use words meaning "several" or "many."

In Chinese the word for "two" is the same as the word for "ears." In the language of Tibet it is the same as the word for "wings." In some languages it is the same as the word for "eyes." Probably the names of most numbers came about in such a way. Our number names came down to us from a very old language. No one knows what they first meant.

In most languages of today the names of all the numbers from 13 to 99 are made from the names of the first ten numbers. "Thirteen" is short for "three and ten," "twenty" for "two tens," and so on. When we pass 99 in counting we have to use the name "hundred." Until we come to a thousand we do not need another name. Then no other new name is needed until we get to a million. Our early ancestors would have had no use for names for very large numbers. But we have. As the need has grown, names such as "billion," "trillion," and "quintillion" have been invented. We could, of course, say "a thousand million," but "billion" is far easier to use.

Inventing a way of counting was one thing. Inventing a way of writing down numbers was quite another. Picture writing was the earliest kind of writing. The American Indians used picture writing until fairly recent times. When an Indian wished to write that ten white men had come in a boat, he put the boat and all ten men in his picture. When he wanted to tell that a journey had taken three days, he put three suns in the picture. But it would not be easy to tell in picture writing that there are about 170 million people in the United States!

One of the earliest ways of writing numbers was to make notches in a stick of wood. Another was to draw short lines on pieces of pottery. In keeping score for games we still often follow the old plan of drawing short lines. We usually group the lines in fives in this way: ⪤⪤ ⪤⪤

The peoples of ancient times all worked out ways of writing numbers. The Egyptians used straight lines for the numbers from one to ten. They used special signs for 100, 1,000, and 10,000.

The ancient Babylonians wrote by pushing little wedge-shaped sticks into tablets of soft clay. Their writing is called cuneiform writing. In their system of numbers 60 was a very important number. They had a special sign for it.

The Greeks used their letters to stand for numbers. They made a special little mark after the letters to show that they were supposed to be numbers and not letters. If we were to write numbers in the Greek way, we would write *a'* for 1, *b'* for 2, and *j'* for 10. Then *k'* would stand for 20, *ka'* for 21, *l'* for 30, and so on.

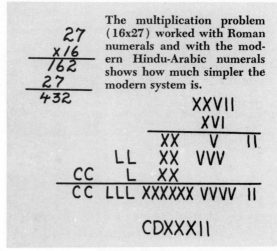

The multiplication problem (16x27) worked with Roman numerals and with the modern Hindu-Arabic numerals shows how much simpler the modern system is.

The Roman signs for the first three numbers were these: I, II, III. Probably they were first just straight lines. The sign for 5 was V. In the beginning it may have been a slanting line across four straight lines. The sign for 4 was IV — 1 from 5. The Romans used the letter X to stand for 10, L for 50, C for 100, D for 500, and M for 1,000. To write any number, therefore, the Romans had to use the letters I, V, X, L, C, D, and M, or combinations of these letters. Arithmetic problems worked in Roman numerals look very bulky and complicated. The picture at the top of the page shows a

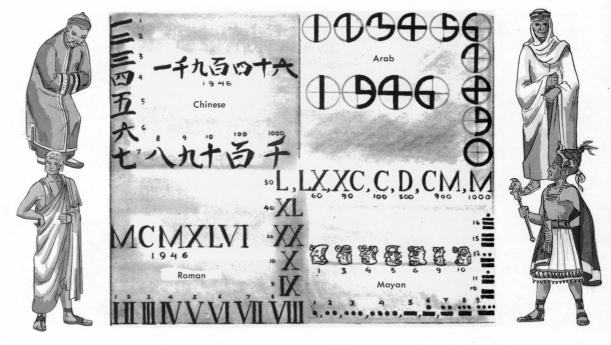

multiplication problem worked out in the Roman way. Beside it is the same problem done in our way of writing numbers.

For centuries the Roman way of writing numbers was used in Europe. It is still used once in a while today. The places where Roman numerals are most often seen now are on book chapters, on cornerstones of buildings, and on the faces of clocks and watches.

But we write most numbers today in signs that came to us from the Arabs. Probably the Arabs did not invent them. They probably got them from the Hindus.

The Hindu-Arab way of writing numbers is far better than any other that has ever been invented. In using it we need only ten different signs. One of those signs is the sign for zero. No older way of writing numbers had a sign for zero.

The big advantage of having a separate sign for zero is that we can use it in combination with the other nine number signs to stand for much larger numbers. Adding one zero after a 5, for instance, makes the number 50. The number 500 is made by adding two zeroes. The Romans had to remember separate signs for 50 and 500.

Arab traders brought their way of writing numbers to Europe during the Middle Ages. These traders came by ship and caravan with costly silks and rugs and spices. Much of their trading was done in the cities of Italy. The Italian merchants probably did not dream that along with the silks and rugs and spices they were getting an invention that was much more important than the goods they bought. But they gradually began to use the invention.

It was, however, nearly four centuries before the Hindu-Arab way of writing numbers was commonly used in Europe. People stubbornly held on to the old Roman numerals. Some people said that the new signs were a heathen invention and should not be used in Christian countries. In Florence, for example, the new numerals were banned by law.

But finally the new numerals won out. People found that it was much easier to write numbers with them than with Roman numerals. They found, too, that it was much easier to add, subtract, multiply, and divide with the new numerals.

Over the centuries as the Hindu-Arab numerals spread from one land to another, they gradually changed in shape. The method of using nine number signs and a zero remained the same, however. Now their use has spread over almost the whole world. (See ABACUS; MATHEMATICS; WRITING; ZERO.)

**NUTS** When we eat a nut, we are eating the seed of a plant. Many nuts—walnuts, almonds, pecans, pistachios, coconuts, and others besides—are the seeds of trees. Some, like the hazelnut, are the seeds of bushes. And some, like the peanut, are the seeds of smaller plants. Nuts have shells around them. The shells of some kinds of nuts are so hard that they have to be cracked open with a hammer.

Some nuts found in American markets come from faraway places. Pistachios come chiefly from the Near East. Many of our almonds come from Mediterranean lands. Cashew nuts are from East Africa and In-

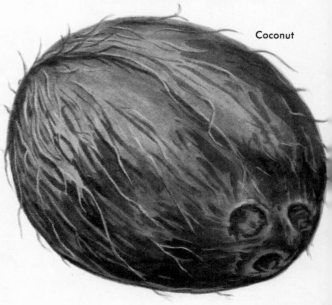

Coconut

Walnut

dia. Brazil nuts come from Brazil. Coconut palms grow on the shores of islands in the Pacific. Some almonds and many pecans, English walnuts, and peanuts are raised in America. Hazelnuts, black walnuts, and hickory nuts grow wild. There were once many chestnut trees, but most of them were killed by a plant disease.

Nuts were probably one of the chief foods of our early ancestors. We roast some of the nuts we eat, but many of them are good raw. They make good food. Since they have fat and protein in them, they can be used instead of meat.

In places where nuts grow wild, nutting time is fun. The nuts are usually ripe in the fall. Outside their hard shell, as a rule, they have a soft green hull. This green hull must be taken off. Squirrels store up nuts

Peanuts

Brazil Nut

Almond

Pecan

for winter food. Gathering nuts sometimes means racing with the squirrels.

Not all the nuts raised and gathered are eaten. The oil pressed from several kinds of nuts is used in soaps and cosmetics. And the famous scientist George Washington Carver found dozens of uses for the peanut. (See CARVER, GEORGE WASHINGTON; FOODS; SOAP.)

**NYALA** In Africa there is a rather large group of hoofed animals known as the "harnessed antelopes." They get their name from white stripes that are arranged so that they look a little like a harness. The nyala is one of the harnessed antelopes. It has a full harness pattern but except in a

There is danger that the nyala will become extinct.

few places the pattern is so blurred that it scarcely shows.

The male nyala has long hair on its neck. It also has a fringe of long hair down its back and another one underneath its body. This long hair makes it look quite different from most antelopes.

Nyalas are scarce. Many antelopes travel in herds, but there are no herds of nyalas. Nyalas are found only in small groups. In fact, there are so few nyalas that they are being carefully protected to keep them from disappearing. (See CONSERVATION; MAMMALS.)

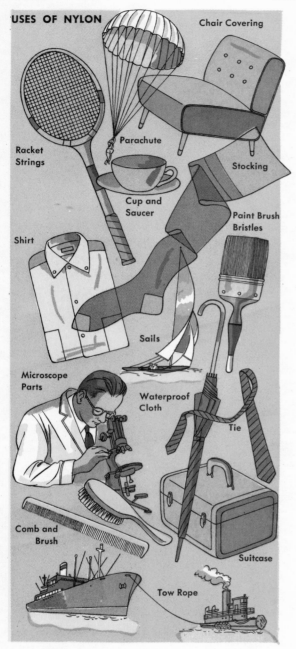

USES OF NYLON

Chair Covering

Parachute

Racket Strings

Stocking

Cup and Saucer

Paint Brush Bristles

Shirt

Sails

Microscope Parts

Waterproof Cloth

Tie

Comb and Brush

Suitcase

Tow Rope

The word "nylon" does not come from any older words. The inventors of the new material made it up. They wanted a name that was short and easy to say.

People first read and heard about nylon in 1938. But the first nylon stockings—stockings were the first things nylon was used for—were not sold until 1940. They were popular at once. People liked them because they were as pretty as silk stockings and lasted longer. Besides, they dried very fast after they were washed. Soon nylon became popular for underwear, too, and for blouses and dresses.

Clothing made of nylon not only dries fast, but better yet, it does not have to be ironed. Nylon dries quickly because no water soaks into the threads themselves. Only enough time is needed for the water sticking to the threads to evaporate.

During World War II new clothing made of nylon was scarce, for most of the nylon made was used for parachutes. But soon after the war it became very common.

Today corncobs have largely taken the place of coal in the making of nylon. In making the fibers a thick liquid is first produced. It looks much like molasses. Great heat and pressure are needed to make it. The liquid is spread out in thin sheets to cool. It hardens, and the sheets are broken up into chips. The chips are then melted, and the liquid is pushed through tiny holes in a metal plate. It comes out as fine threads which soon cool and harden. Several threads are twisted together to make "yarn" for weaving. The yarn is then stretched to make the threads strong.

Not all the nylon being made now is used for fibers for cloth. Many brushes now have nylon bristles. Surgeons use nylon threads to sew up wounds. Tennis racquets may be strung with nylon, and fishing lines are made of it. It is also used for buttons and dish covers and phonograph needles. Some machines have parts made of nylon. (See FIBERS; PARACHUTES; PLASTICS; SPINNING AND WEAVING.)

**NYLON** In early days and even not long ago, people wove all their cloth from fibers they got from plants and animals—such fibers as silk, wool, cotton, and linen. Now scientists have learned how to make fibers of many kinds. It seems a miracle that some of these fibers can be made out of the materials that are used. Nylon is one of these miracle fibers. The inventors of nylon made it from coal, air, and water!

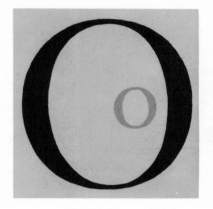

The letter O began as the picture of the human eye (👁). This eye looks down from the hieroglyphics on many an Egyptian tomb or temple wall. The makers of the first alphabet borrowed the picture to serve as a letter.

Before long the letter was drawn more simply ( O ). And for 3,000 years its shape has changed very little.

O has many different sounds. It has different sounds in these words: *no, do, worm, boy, wolf, soft, not, some, women,* and *lord.* Sometimes, moreover, it is silent, as in *button.*

O is one of the few letters which is a whole word.

**OAKS** "As sturdy as an oak" is a common saying. It is a wise one, too, for oaks are sturdy plants that can stand many hardships. Most oaks are trees, some 150 feet tall, but a few are bushes. There are at least 75 different kinds of oaks in the United States.

Oaks are sturdy partly because they grow slowly. An old Danish legend tells about a count who persuaded an enemy who had captured him to let him plant and harvest just one more crop on his land. The seeds the count planted were the seeds of oak trees. The trees were not ready to be harvested for their lumber for many, many years.

Oak wood is hard and durable. It is an especially good wood for furniture and for shipbuilding. The bark of some oak trees is used in tanning leather. Cork comes from the bark of the cork oak, which grows chiefly in Spain.

All oaks produce acorns. Each acorn is a seed with a hard covering around it. Each one has a cup at the top. Squirrels and many other animals eat acorns. People sometimes eat them, too.

The flowers of oak trees usually appear before the trees leaf out in the spring. Each oak tree has two kinds of flowers. One has stamens. The other has pistils. The flowers are not showy like garden flowers, but without the flowers there would be no acorns.

Most oak trees lose their leaves in the fall and get new ones in the spring. But there are some evergreen oaks. The live oaks of southern United States, for instance, are green all the year round. These live oaks are often draped with long moss.

Their leaves and their acorns are a big help in telling oak trees apart. The pictures show the leaves and acorns of two of the oaks of America.

There are many famous oak trees. The Charter Oak, for instance, played an important part in Connecticut's early history. The colony's charter was hidden in it for a time. (See BARK; CORK; FORESTS AND FORESTRY; GALLS; LUMBERING; TREES.)

Scarlet Oak Leaf

Scarlet Oak Acorn

Leaf

Acorn

California Live Oak

**OBELISK** The people of ancient Egypt built many monuments. Some of their monuments were obelisks. An obelisk is a solid four-sided shaft of stone cut from a single block of stone. At the top it has a pyramid. The Egyptians made the pyramids of their obelisks shine by covering them with electrum, a mixture of silver and gold.

There is now an obelisk in Central Park in New York City. It was given to the United States by Egypt in 1890. There is one much like it in London. These two obelisks are called "Cleopatra's Needles." They are named in honor of Cleopatra, a famous queen of Egypt. But they were made long before her time. They were made during the 15th century B.C. to honor the pharaoh Thutmose III. The "needles" were moved to Alexandria while Cleopatra was queen. Then, almost 2,000 years later, they came to New York and London.

The largest obelisk that remains from the days of ancient Egypt is in Rome. It is 105 feet, 9 inches tall. This obelisk was taken to Rome by Constantine the Great.

The Washington Monument in Washington, D.C., has the same shape as the obelisks of ancient Egypt, but it is several times larger than they were. And it is not a solid shaft cut from one block of stone. (See EGYPT; WASHINGTON MONUMENT.)

**OCEANS** More than two-thirds of the earth is covered with water. Most of this water is in four great oceans. Of these oceans the Pacific is by far the largest. It is also the deepest. The chart below shows how the other oceans compare with it.

| OCEAN | AREA IN SQ. MI. | AVERAGE DEPTH IN FT. | GREATEST DEPTH IN FT. |
|---|---|---|---|
| Pacific | 63,800,000 | 14,050 | 35,948 |
| Atlantic | 31,830,000 | 12,880 | 30,246 |
| Indian | 28,357,000 | 13,000 | 24,440 |
| Arctic | 5,440,000 | 4,200 | 17,850 |

The water of all the oceans is salty. Many clever stories have been made up to explain why. But only this story is true: Rivers are constantly pouring water into the oceans. Some of this water in its journey to the sea gets salt from the rocks it flows over. It does not get enough to make it taste salty. But for millions and millions of years rivers have been bringing salt to the seas. All these years water has been evaporating from the seas leaving the salt behind. Century by century the oceans have become more and more salty.

There are many other minerals in ocean water, too. One scientist has figured that in the oceans there are 830 million tons of gold! But it would cost more to take it out of the oceans than it would be worth.

**CURRENTS OF THE WORLD'S OCEANS**

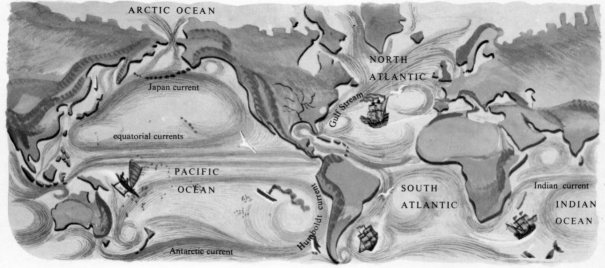

The oceans furnish us with huge amounts of food. Much of it is fish. If we could count all the fish in the oceans, the number would be so big that not many people could read it. Besides the fish, there are shrimps and lobsters and crabs. There are oysters and scallops. In some parts of the world people eat octopuses, sea cucumbers *(bêche-de-mer)*, and sea worms, too.

There are still other things that we get from the great storehouse of the sea. Whale oil, sponges, pearls, and kelp are examples.

In the oceans there are great streams called currents. Some are warm; some are cold. They have much to do with the climate of the lands they flow by.

Today the seas of the world are great highways. Ships go back and forth over them carrying goods of many kinds from land to land. (See ARCTIC OCEAN; ATLANTIC OCEAN; DEEP-SEA EXPLORING; FISHING; INDIAN OCEAN; PACIFIC OCEAN; SHIPS; TIDES.)

**OCTOPUS** With its long snakelike arms, its soft body, and its big eyes, the octopus is anything but a handsome creature. The octopus is, moreover, a fierce fighter. No wonder it is often called the devilfish!

Even though it lives in water, the octopus is not a fish. Instead, it belongs to the great group of animals called mollusks. But in one way it is very different from most of its mollusk relatives. Almost all mollusks have shells. The octopus has no shell at all.

An octopus has eight arms. Its name comes from the Greek words meaning "eight" and "feet." On each of the arms there are two rows of suckers. The octopus can certainly hold on tight to anything it has in its arms. Its arms help it catch other animals for food. It catches chiefly crabs. First it paralyzes a crab by sending a poison into its body. Then it pulls the crab to pieces with its mouth and arms.

Octopuses are animals of the warm seas. They hide among the corals there.

The octopus uses its eight arms to catch food.

Often they find a dark crack or cavern. But it is easy for them to hide even where it is not dark. They can change their color to match their surroundings so that they are hard to see. If there is real danger, octopuses are able to send out from their bodies an inky fluid that makes a smoke screen for them.

Like its relatives the squids, an octopus swims by shooting itself backward. It has a tube, or funnel, through which water can be forced out of its body. It moves by a kind of jet propulsion. The eight arms of an octopus are joined together at the base to make an "umbrella." An octopus can also glide backward by opening and closing its umbrella, and it can crawl forward on its arms.

There are octopuses of about 50 different kinds. Most of them are too small to be dangerous to people. The only truly dangerous one is the giant octopus of the Pacific Ocean. Its spread-out arms may measure 20 feet across.

A mother octopus places each of her eggs in a capsule and fastens it to a rock. She stays near the eggs till they hatch. A baby octopus looks like its parents except that it is much smaller.

Octopuses are eaten by the people of some countries. In fact, in Japan and Italy they are considered very choice food. Canned octopus can be bought in America in cities. (See INK; MOLLUSKS; SQUIDS.)

**OHIO** Midway between the Midwest and the Northeast is the rather small state of Ohio. It is crowded with people. Factories and farms, museums and laboratories, Indian mounds and old-time villages, presidents and inventors—all are a part of the story of the "Buckeye State."

The first white men who came into the Ohio country saw a few patches of open prairie and large areas of thick forest. In these forests, among the oak, hickory, and walnut trees, there were many buckeyes. The buckeyes have since been cut down along with most of the other trees, but the nickname "Buckeye State" remains.

In 1788 the first Ohio settlement was made at Marietta on the Ohio River. The settlers were New England war veterans. They built a village of sturdy blockhouses. Many settlers followed them.

In 1796 Moses Cleaveland and a company of Connecticut men founded Cleveland on the shore of Lake Erie. Settlement of other land along Lake Erie followed. This land is called the Western Reserve.

Settlers continued to come both by way of the Ohio River and the Great Lakes. They cleared land for farming and built villages and cities with mills and factories. They worked the coal mines and dug the clay. In a very few years Ohio was ready to be admitted to the Union. In 1803 it became the 17th state.

Ohio kept on growing. During the Canal Age, 1825-1850, two Ohio canals connected the Ohio River with Lake Erie. Ohio had some of the earliest railroads in the country. In the early 1900's many places were connected by electric railways. They, like the canals, are no longer used. Now, however, the main railroad lines between East and West cross Ohio. Rail, lake, river, air, and roadway furnish Ohio with good transportation. Ohio expects to gain in many ways from the recently completed St. Lawrence Seaway.

Today only four states have more people than Ohio. People from almost every country in Europe have come to Ohio to work. It is second to New York State in the money made by manufacturing. Ohio has eight cities of more than 100,000. They do not have all the industry. Some of the largest factories are in small cities and towns. Many Ohioans divide their time between crop raising and factory jobs.

When skies above Cleveland, Youngstown, or Canton glow with flames one knows that the iron and steel mills are at work. Akron is the "rubber capital." Toledo, a great coal port, is also a big glassmaking center. Cincinnati, Dayton, and Columbus have large factories of many kinds.

Thriving farms still place Ohio among the top 12 states in the value of the crops raised. Much of its land is badly eroded and much of its soil is worn out. But the farmers, by using new methods, are growing bumper crops again. Dairying is the chief farm business.

Cleveland is the center of a great sprawling group of suburbs and other cities. It advertises that it has "the best location in the nation." Its growing industries point to the truth of the advertisement. The whole state lives up to its name, Ohio, an Indian word meaning "great."

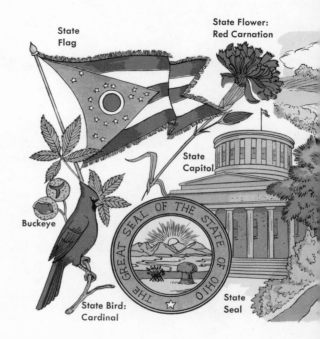

State Flag

State Flower: Red Carnation

State Capitol

Buckeye

State Bird: Cardinal

State Seal

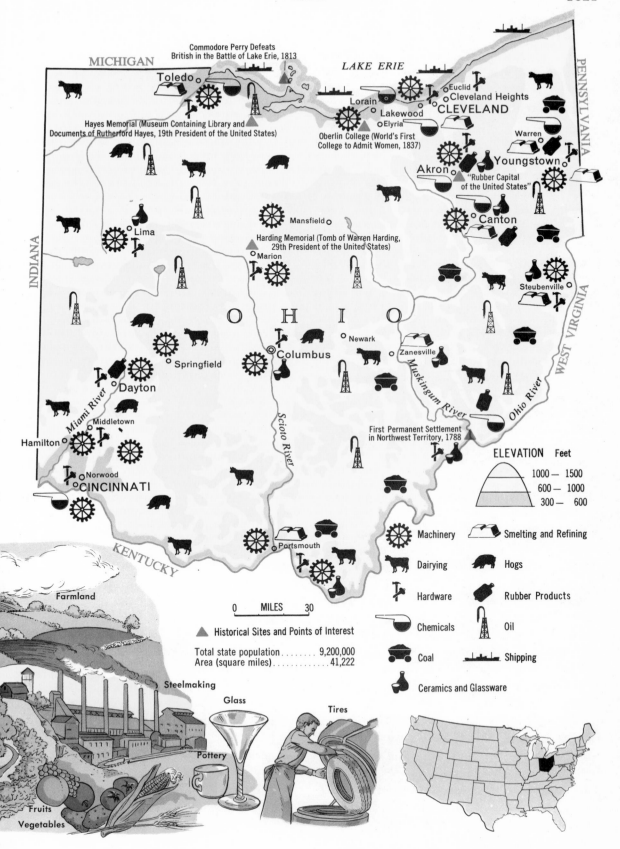

MICHIGAN

Commodore Perry Defeats
British in the Battle of Lake Erie, 1813

LAKE ERIE

Toledo

Euclid
Cleveland Heights
CLEVELAND
Lorain
Lakewood
Elyria

Warren

Hayes Memorial (Museum Containing Library and
Documents of Rutherford Hayes, 19th President of the United States)

Oberlin College (World's First
College to Admit Women, 1837)

Youngstown

Akron
"Rubber Capital
of the United States"

PENNSYLVANIA

INDIANA

Lima

Mansfield

Canton

Harding Memorial (Tomb of Warren Harding,
29th President of the United States)

Marion

Steubenville

O  H  I  O

Newark

Springfield

Columbus

Zanesville

WEST VIRGINIA

Dayton

Muskingum River

Miami River

Middletown

Scioto River

Ohio River

Hamilton

First Permanent Settlement
in Northwest Territory, 1788

Norwood
CINCINNATI

ELEVATION  Feet

1000 — 1500
600 — 1000
300 — 600

Portsmouth

KENTUCKY

Machinery          Smelting and Refining

Dairying           Hogs

Hardware           Rubber Products

0  MILES  30

Chemicals          Oil

▲ Historical Sites and Points of Interest

Coal               Shipping

Total state population........ 9,200,000
Area (square miles)............41,222

Ceramics and Glassware

Farmland

Steelmaking

Glass

Tires

Pottery

Fruits

Vegetables

**OKLAHOMA** This southern Great Plains state is one of the later comers to the Union. It did not become a state until 1907. A few people living today can remember the excitement of the opening up of Oklahoma for white settlement. Stories have been written about it and movies made that show how, on April 22, 1889, at the shot of a gun, homesteaders rushed across the boundary. They came on horseback, on muleback, in covered wagons, on bicycles, and even on foot to stake out claims to the free land. Their wagons bulged with household goods, plows, and bags of grain for seed. Within 24 hours there were about 50,000 settlers. Within a few days towns such as Guthrie and Oklahoma City had as many as 10,000 people each.

To see how this came about one needs to look back to the days when most of Oklahoma was the Indian Territory. It was the home of Indian tribes who had lost their homes in the East. The United States Government gave them the land to have "as long as grass shall grow and rivers run." The Indians did well in farming and trading until the days of the War between the States. Their warriors fought on the side of the South. Afterward the United States Government felt that the Indians had lost all rights to their lands. Finally it was agreed that white settlers would be kept out, but that other Indian tribes would be allowed in the territory. One chief was asked, "What will you call your territory?" He replied, "Oklahoma." *Okla* meant "people," and *homa* meant "red."

The regions bordering the Oklahoma Territory were filling with white settlers. In 1879 they began demanding that certain parts of Oklahoma be opened for white settlement. Ten years later, after the government had made an arrangement with the Indians, came the opening.

Oklahoma grew rapidly. In 1890, there were about 140,000 people there. In 1957, when the state was 50 years old, there were almost 16 times as many. Since it is a

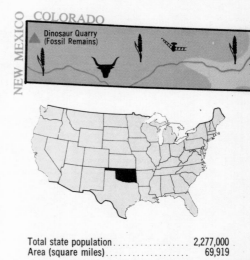

| | |
|---|---|
| Total state population | 2,277,000 |
| Area (square miles) | 69,919 |

rather large state, it is not crowded. About half the people live in cities.

In Indian days Oklahoma was grazing land. Today the raising of livestock is a big business on the high plains of the west and in the mountains of the southeast. The other vast open ranges are now divided into well-fenced farms. Wheat is the main crop in the north, corn in the center, and cotton in the south.

A second big boom came to Oklahoma when its rich oil fields were tapped shortly after it became a state. Some Indians are among those who have grown rich on Oklahoma's "liquid gold." Oklahoma is one of the four leading states in oil production.

Tulsa and Oklahoma City, the two cities with over 100,000 people each, are large oil centers. Tulsa is called the "oil capital of the world." Several of the large oil companies have their main offices there. The oil fields and refineries are on the outskirts of the city. Oil was also found directly under Oklahoma City; pumps stand right among the buildings. Both Oklahoma City and Tulsa also have aircraft plants, stockyards, meat-packing plants, flour mills, and factories for making machinery for oil fields and refineries.

Among special events in Oklahoma is Will Rogers Day. The people are proud that the famous humorist was born in the state of Oklahoma.

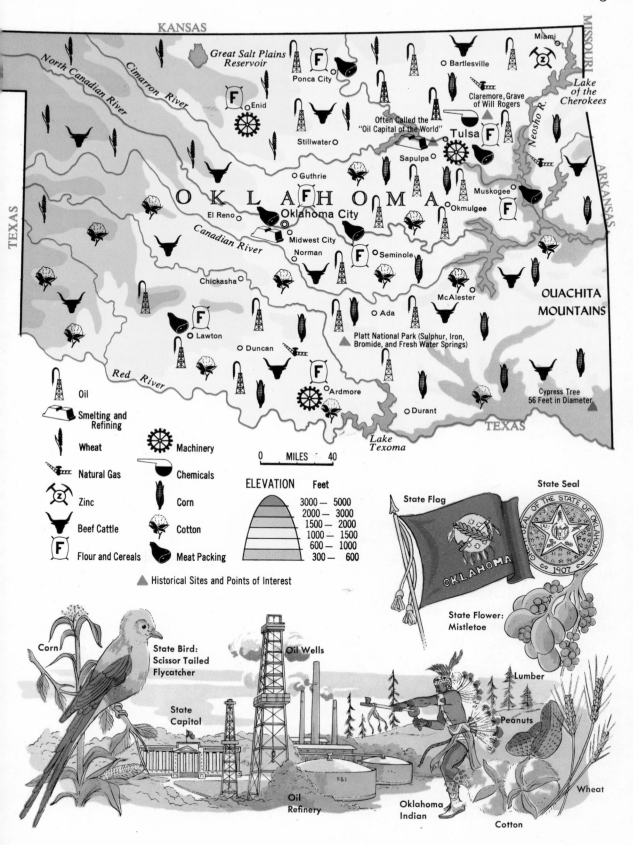

KANSAS

North Canadian River

Cimarron River

Great Salt Plains Reservoir

Ponca City

Enid

Bartlesville

Miami

Claremore, Grave of Will Rogers

Neosho R.

Lake of the Cherokees

Often Called the "Oil Capital of the World"

Tulsa

Stillwater

Sapulpa

Muskogee

Guthrie

O K L A H O M A

Okmulgee

El Reno

Oklahoma City

Midwest City

Canadian River

Norman

Seminole

TEXAS

ARKANSAS

Chickasha

McAlester

OUACHITA MOUNTAINS

Ada

Lawton

Platt National Park (Sulphur, Iron, Bromide, and Fresh Water Springs)

Duncan

Red River

Ardmore

Durant

Cypress Tree 56 Feet in Diameter

Lake Texoma

TEXAS

## Legend

Oil

Smelting and Refining

Wheat

Machinery

Natural Gas

Chemicals

Zinc

Corn

Beef Cattle

Cotton

Flour and Cereals

Meat Packing

▲ Historical Sites and Points of Interest

0   MILES   40

| ELEVATION | Feet |
|---|---|
| 3000 — | 5000 |
| 2000 — | 3000 |
| 1500 — | 2000 |
| 1000 — | 1500 |
| 600 — | 1000 |
| 300 — | 600 |

State Flag

State Seal

GREAT SEAL OF THE STATE OF OKLAHOMA 1907

OKLAHOMA

State Flower: Mistletoe

Corn

State Bird: Scissor Tailed Flycatcher

Oil Wells

Lumber

State Capitol

Peanuts

581

Oil Refinery

Oklahoma Indian

Cotton

Wheat

CHANGES IN THE UNITED STATES FLAG

First United States Flag
1777

Cambridge Flag
1775

Star Spangled Banner
1814

United States Flag
1912-1959

Great Star Flag
1818

Mexican War Flag
1846

Thirteen Stripe Flag
1818

**OLD GLORY** The United States flag has several nicknames. One of the best-known nicknames is Old Glory. The pictures above trace the history of the United States flag.

The Cambridge flag was used in the early days of the Revolutionary War. The small British flag in the corner showed that the colonies were still linked to Britain.

The first United States flag, approved by Congress in 1777, had 13 stripes (seven red and six white) and 13 stars in a blue field. By 1814, two more states had entered the Union, and two more stripes and two more stars had been added to the flag.

There were 20 states in the Union and 20 stars in the flag by 1818. The number of stripes, however, was reduced to 13. Some of the 1818 flags were called Great Star Flags because they had the 20 stars arranged in the form of one big star.

The flag carried during the Mexican War (1846-48) had 28 stars. In 1912 the number of states and stars reached 48. No new stars were added until 1959, when the entrance of both Alaska and Hawaii brought the total of states to 50.

**"OLD IRONSIDES"** One of the most famous ships of the United States Navy was nicknamed "Old Ironsides." It was named the "Constitution" when it was built. It was a frigate—a sailing vessel.

The "Constitution" was launched in 1797. It was made of wood and had 44 guns.

This ship was in 40 battles and was never defeated. It could outsail every ship it met. Some of the battles it fought were with pirate ships. Others were with English ships during the War of 1812.

In 1830 the United States Navy decided that the ship was ready for the scrap heap. But Oliver Wendell Holmes, an American poet, did not like the idea at all. He thought that the ship should be saved. He wrote a poem called "Old Ironsides" to say so.

A great many people read it and agreed with the poet. They gave money for putting "Old Ironsides" into good shape again. In the next 25 years the ship went on many cruises. Then it was tied up in a navy yard.

In 1927 the school children of the United States collected pennies to put "Old Ironsides" into good shape once more. With the pennies and some money Congress gave, the ship was made into a floating museum. Every year thousands of visitors to Boston visit "Old Ironsides," which is now in the navy yard there. (See NAVY.)

"Old Ironsides"

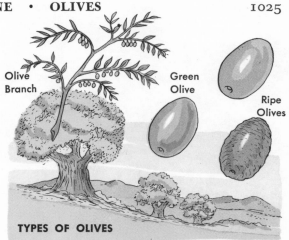

**TYPES OF OLIVES**

Olive Branch

Green Olive

Ripe Olives

**OLEOMARGARINE** Most people cannot tell oleomargarine from butter. It looks like butter and tastes like it, too. It is mostly fat, just as butter is. But the fat does not come from cream as the fat from butter does. It may come from beef suet or pork lard. Margarine much like that made from animal fats may be made from the oil in cottonseed, corn, or coconuts. It may be made from the oil in soybeans or peanuts, or from still other vegetable oils. Skim milk added to the fat used helps to give margarine a taste like butter.

Margarine is colored to make it yellow. For a time in the United States there was a heavy tax on margarine that was colored before it was sold. Most people therefore bought it uncolored and added the coloring themselves. Now the heavy tax has been taken off, and the makers add the coloring.

Butter used to be considered a better food than margarine because it had more vitamins in it. Now vitamins are being added to margarine so that it will be just as nourishing a food as butter.

Margarine is a much newer food than butter. It was first made in France less than 100 years ago. During a time when there was a food shortage in France, the French government offered a prize to anyone who could make a good substitute for butter. A French scientist won the prize by making oleomargarine from beef suet. Now most margarine comes from vegetable oils. (See BUTTER; FOODS; VITAMINS.)

**OLIVES** For several thousand years trees like those in the pictures have been a common sight in Mediterranean lands. They are olive trees. In ancient Greece a branch of an olive tree was used as a sign of peace. The winners in the Olympic games were given crowns of olive leaves.

Olive trees keep on growing even during the hot, dry summers of lands near the Mediterranean. Their long roots take in moisture from deep in the ground. Their small silvery-green leaves do not lose water as fast as large leaves would. These trees grow especially well in soil made up mostly of ash from volcanoes. Some old olive trees have trunks more than five feet across.

Olive trees bear for centuries. An old saying is that a man who plants olive trees plants wealth for his great-grandchildren.

Raising olive trees has now spread from Mediterranean countries to many other parts of the world. Some olives are raised in southwestern United States.

Millions of bottles of pickled olives are sold every year. Both green olives and ripe olives are pickled. But the most important food from olive trees has always been olive oil. The best olive oil is pressed out of olives that are not quite ripe. Olive oil is used in a number of countries instead of butter in cooking. In even more places this oil is used in making salad dressing.

Much olive oil also goes into the making of fine soap. The wood of the olive tree is sometimes used in furniture.

Olive Gathering

ANCIENT OLYMPICS

Chariot Races

Javelin

Discus
Throwing

Boxing

Wrestling

Foot Races

**OLYMPIC GAMES** More than 2,500 years ago in Greece people gathered every four years at a place called Olympia to watch and take part in athletic games. In the beginning the games were made up only of short foot races. At the very first there was only one race, the "Stade." The word "stadium" comes from its name. The first victor we have a record of was Coroebus, a cook from Elis. Soon other races were added. The games were part of a celebration at the temple of Zeus.

Gradually other contests were included. Besides the foot races, there were wrestling and boxing matches, jumping, discus and javelin throwing, chariot races, and other kinds of sports. Sometimes the games lasted as long as five days.

In time the Olympic games became a great festival for all of Greece. Any fighting between the city-states ceased and a sacred truce was proclaimed for the opening of the festival. Men came together from all parts of the Greek world. When they saw what fine athletes there were in all the city-states, they were proud to be Greeks.

Each winner in the games was crowned with a wreath of olive leaves. The winners were regarded as great heroes. Often statues were erected to them in their native cities, and they held a place of honor in all public celebrations. The Greek calendar was divided into "Olympiads," the four-year periods between the games.

The Olympic games in Greece ended more than 1,500 years ago. But the games were started again in 1896. The first modern Olympics were held in Athens, Greece. Since then they have been held every four years, just as the Greek games were, except during the two world wars. Two were held in the United States: in St. Louis, in 1904, and in Los Angeles, in 1932.

The modern Olympic games last more than two weeks. They include many of the same events the ancient Greeks had in their games. In addition there are water sports, cycling, fencing, horseback riding, weight lifting, and gymnastics. Sports such as basketball, water polo, football, and hockey are often added. A sport must be practiced in at least 20 countries in order to be included in the modern Olympic games.

The opening ceremony of the Olympics is very impressive. Important parts of it are the parade of athletes and the arrival of the Olympic Flame. In the parade the athletes of each nation march by the reviewing stand accompanied by the flag of their nation. The countries are in alphabetical order in the parade with two exceptions: The group from Greece always leads the parade. The group from the country where the games are being held is always last.

After the parade there is a great fanfare of trumpets and a runner appears bearing a lighted torch — the Olympic Flame. The "Sacred Fire" is then lit. It burns until the games are over.

Winter games were started in 1924. They are held at a different time of year and in a different city from the regular games. The winter games include skiing, skating, bobsledding, and ice hockey.

The 1956 regular Olympic games were held in Melbourne, Australia. Five thousand athletes from 67 countries took part in them. The team from the Soviet Union won the most points in these games; the United States came second. As the Greek games brought together the people from different cities, so the Olympic games today help people of different countries to know and understand one another better.

**OMNIVOROUS ANIMALS** Some animals eat only meat. Some eat only plants. Others eat both plants and animals. Those that eat both are called omnivorous animals. "Omnivorous" means "all-eating."

People are omnivorous animals. A good diet calls for meat as well as for fruits and vegetables. Many birds, many monkeys, and some bears are also among the omnivorous animals. (See CARNIVOROUS ANIMALS; HERBIVOROUS ANIMALS.)

MODERN OLYMPICS

Field and Ice Hockey

Olympic Banner

Torch

Swimming and Diving

Hammer Throw

Winter Sports

Baseball and Basketball

Pole Vaulting

Weight Lifting

Horseback Riding

Pistol Shooting

Track

Fencing

A Scene from *Hänsel and Gretel*

**OPERA** The picture above shows a scene from the opera *Hänsel and Gretel*. In an opera a story is acted out just as in a play. But in an opera most, and often all, of the words are sung, not spoken.

*Hänsel and Gretel* is based on one of Grimm's fairy tales. Hänsel and Gretel are the son and daughter of a poor broommaker. They go to hunt for strawberries and get lost in the woods. A wicked witch who lives in a candy house surrounded by a gingerbread fence captures them, but they manage to escape. This opera was written by Engelbert Humperdinck. He wrote it for his sister's children.

Operas are divided into acts and scenes just as plays are. An opera usually calls for many singers. The singers of the chief parts need powerful voices as well as beautiful ones, for most opera houses are big. Other singers make up the chorus. An opera calls for a big stage, much scenery, and many costumes. Besides the singers there are often "supers." They have no words to sing, but they are in costume and help to make scenes seem real.

A ballet makes up a part of many operas. An opera company must have a corps of ballet dancers. An opera company must have a big orchestra, too. In every opera there is some music without any singing. Before the curtain goes up, for instance, the orchestra plays an overture.

*Aïda* is a much more elaborate opera than *Hänsel and Gretel*. *Aïda* was written by the Italian composer Giuseppe Verdi. It tells the story of an Egyptian princess (Amneris), an Ethiopian slave who was a captive princess (Aïda), and a captain of the Egyptian guards (Rhadames). In this opera there are four acts divided into several scenes. In addition to the chief characters there are priests, priestesses, soldiers, slaves, dancers, prisoners of war, and crowds of Egyptian people. In the second act Rhadames returns home from an expedition with many prisoners he has captured. He is honored by the king of Egypt with a triumphal procession. The stage is crowded and the costumes are splendid. The music for the procession is the "Grand March." No wonder operas like *Aïda* are often called "grand" operas.

Many people who have never been in an opera house and have never seen an opera know a great deal of music that comes from operas. The "Grand March" from *Aïda* is often played. The "Soldiers' Chorus" from *Faust*, the "Wedding March" from *Lohengrin*, and the "Toreador Song" from

*Carmen* are a few of the other bits of opera that millions of people know.

Another well-known bit of opera is the *William Tell* overture. The story of the famous Swiss patriot was made into an opera by the Italian composer Gioacchino Rossini. The chief melody of its overture is used as the theme song for the "Lone Ranger" on radio and television.

For the beginnings of opera one must go back to the 16th century. A group of scholars and musicians in the Italian city of Florence decided to combine drama and music. One of the members of this group was Vincenzo Galilei, the father of the famous scientist Galileo.

The oldest opera still performed today was first produced a little over 350 years ago. It is *Orfeo,* by the Italian composer Claudio Monteverdi.

Many Italian operas heard today were composed by Verdi. Verdi would be famous if he had written nothing but *Aïda,* but he also wrote *Rigoletto, Il Trovatore (The Troubadour), La Traviata (The Lost Lady), Otello,* and *Falstaff.* The last two of these are based on plays by Shakespeare.

The foremost Italian composer of our century was Giacomo Puccini (poot CHEE nee). He wrote *La Bohème (The Bohemians), Tosca,* and *Madame Butterfly.* Gian-Carlo Menotti is another modern Italian composer. His best-known work is *Amahl and the Night Visitors,* which has been given several times on television at Christmas time. It is the story of a crippled boy and the Wise Men who were on their way to take gifts to the baby Jesus.

*Faust* and *Carmen* are two of the most popular operas. They were both written by French composers. Charles Gounod wrote *Faust.* Georges Bizet wrote *Carmen.*

The first important German opera composer was Wolfgang Amadeus Mozart. He wrote *The Marriage of Figaro, Don Giovanni, The Magic Flute,* and other operas. Many people think that *Don Giovanni* is the finest of all operas.

SOME FAMOUS OPERAS

Tannhäuser

Lohengrin

Amahl and the Night Visitors

Rigoletto

Otello

Marriage of Figaro

The greatest German opera composers after Mozart were Ludwig van Beethoven and Richard Wagner. Beethoven wrote only one opera, *Fidelio*. Wagner wrote many operas. He called his operas "music dramas." Among his best-known operas are *Tannhäuser, Lohengrin,* and the four operas called *The Ring of the Nibelungs.*

A later German composer was Richard Strauss. Strauss' *Der Rosenkavalier (The Cavalier of the Roses)* contains some of the most beautiful waltzes ever written.

One of the most famous Russian operas is *Boris Godunov,* by Modest Musorgski. It tells the story of a Russian czar. Musorgski used Russian folk songs, folk dances, and church music in this opera. *The Love of Three Oranges* is a modern Russian opera by Sergei Prokofiev, the composer of *Peter and the Wolf.*

Not many English or American operas have been successful. There are several rather new American operas. One is *Vanessa,* by Samuel Barber. Another is *Susannah,* by Carlisle Floyd. It is too early to tell whether these operas will last.

The famous operas are sung year after year. In the United States, operas are usually sung in the language in which they were originally written. Although many of those who go to an opera cannot understand the words that are sung, they can understand the story from the acting.

Great opera stars have come from all over the world. Caruso, who is sometimes called the greatest of all opera singers, was an Italian. Feodor Chaliapin was Russian. Nellie Melba came from Australia, Mary Garden from Scotland, Kirsten Flagstad from Norway, Lily Pons from France, and Maria Jeritza from Austria. And today there are many American stars.

One of the world's most famous opera houses is *La Scala.* It is in Milan, Italy. The *Opéra* in Paris, Covent Garden in London, and the Metropolitan Opera House in New York City are three of the other world-famous opera houses.

**OPERETTA** "Light opera" is another name for operetta. Like an opera, an operetta is a play set to music. But an operetta, as a rule, does not need as big a stage, or as big a theater, or as big an orchestra as an opera needs. It does not need such big voices, either. Besides, many operas are tragic; they have sad endings. Most operettas are gay and have happy endings. Another important difference is that in an operetta many of the words are spoken instead of sung.

In one type of operetta called musical comedy, a great deal of emphasis is put on the plot. The songs and dances help the audience understand the feelings of the people in the play. They are not just pleasant "interruptions," as they often are in other types of operetta.

Gilbert and Sullivan made up one of the most famous teams in the history of operetta. Gilbert wrote the words and Sullivan wrote the music for about a dozen operettas. *The Mikado* and *H.M.S. Pinafore* are two of the best known.

Rodgers and Hammerstein make up a famous team of musical comedy writers. Rodgers writes the music and Hammerstein the words, or lyrics. *Oklahoma!* and *South Pacific* are two musical comedies we owe to this team.

The list on the next page names some of the famous operetta composers. It also gives the names of the operettas that made them famous.

Some of the operettas in the list are played season after season. Others are seldom heard, but some of the songs from them live on.

The picture at the bottom of the next page shows a scene from *Oklahoma!* This operetta has been sung year after year since it was first produced in 1943. Although the picture cannot tell anything about the music, it does give an idea of the colorful setting and gay costumes that have helped to make this operetta so popular. (See GILBERT AND SULLIVAN; MUSIC.)

## FAMOUS OPERETTAS

| | |
|---|---|
| John Gay (1685-1732) (words) and John Christopher Pepusch (1667-1752) (arranged music) | *The Beggar's Opera* |
| Johann Strauss (1825-1899) | *Die Fledermaus (The Bat)* |
| Reginald De Koven (1859-1920) | *Robin Hood* |
| Victor Herbert (1859-1924) | *The Fortune Teller* *Babes in Toyland* *The Red Mill* *Naughty Marietta* *Sweethearts* |
| Franz Lehár (1870-1948) | *The Merry Widow* |
| Oskar Straus (1870-1954) | *The Chocolate Soldier* |
| Rudolf Friml (1879-    ) | *Rose Marie* *The Vagabond King* |
| Jerome Kern (1885-1945) | *Show Boat* |
| Sigmund Romberg (1887-1951) | *Maytime* *Blossom Time* *The Student Prince* *The Desert Song* *The New Moon* |
| Irving Berlin (1888-    ) | *Annie Get Your Gun* |
| Cole Porter (1893-    ) | *Kiss Me, Kate* |
| Lorenz Hart (1895-1943) (words) and Richard Rodgers (1902-    ) (music) | *A Connecticut Yankee* *Pal Joey* |
| Oscar Hammerstein II (1895-    ) (words) and Richard Rodgers (1902-    ) (music) | *Oklahoma!* *Carousel* *South Pacific* *The King and I* |
| George Gershwin (1898-1937) | *Of Thee I Sing* *Porgy and Bess* |
| Noel Coward (1899-    ) | *Bittersweet* |
| Frederick Loewe (1904-    ) (music) and Allan Jay Lerner (1918-    ) (words) | *Brigadoon* *Paint Your Wagon* *My Fair Lady* |
| Frank Loesser (1910-    ) | *Guys and Dolls* *The Most Happy Fella* |
| Leonard Bernstein (1918-    ) | *On the Town* *Candide* *West Side Story* |

"Porgy and Bess"

"Annie Get Your Gun"

"Oklahoma!"

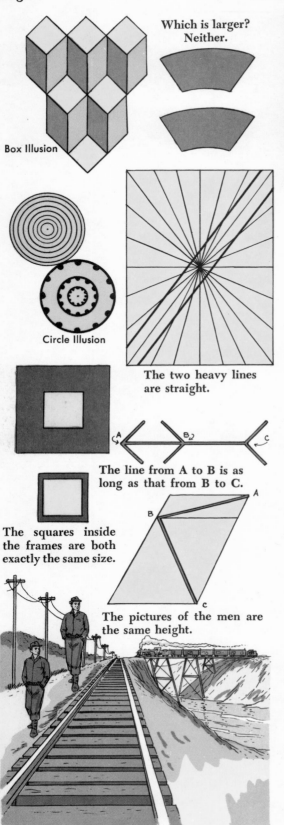

Box Illusion

Which is larger?
Neither.

Circle Illusion

The two heavy lines
are straight.

The line from A to B is as
long as that from B to C.

The squares inside
the frames are both
exactly the same size.

The pictures of the men are
the same height.

**OPTICAL ILLUSIONS** "Seeing is be-
lieving" is a common saying. But it is not
always a good one. Our eyes can play
strange tricks on us. The tricks our eyes
play on us are called optical illusions. The
pictures show a few examples.

In the box illusion, most people see five
boxes when they first glance at it. But if
stared at for a time, the picture shifts and
there are only three boxes.

For the circle illusion one must slowly
turn the book and stare at the centers of
the circles. One seems to spin in one direction and the other in the opposite direction.

The pictures of the men in the drawing
at the bottom of the page are both exactly
the same size. The second man, however,
looks like a giant. We normally expect the
second man to look smaller because he is
farther away. The railroad track is drawn
as it would really look to us. Of course, we
know that the rails do not actually come
together in the distance as they appear to.

Water creates some optical illusions by
making things seem to be where they are
not. Light rays from an object under water
usually bend as they leave the water. This
bending causes an illusion. If the Indian
in the picture throws his spear at the fish
where it seems to be, he will miss it.

Architects, home decorators, and dress
designers often make use of optical illusions. Vertical patterns on wall paper, for
example, make a ceiling look higher.

The size of the full moon as it rises is
one of the commonest optical illusions.

The moon seems to be much larger when it is rising than when it is overhead. Photographs of the full moon low in the sky are always disappointing because the moon looks too small. The moon can fool our eyes, but it cannot fool a camera. Many optical illusions are easy to explain, but not the moon illusion. Scientists have been trying to explain it for 2,000 years. (See CAMOUFLAGE; LIGHT; MIRAGE; PROTECTIVE COLORING.)

**ORACLES** Will this child grow up to be healthy, wealthy, and wise? Will this new venture turn out well? What important happenings will take place soon?

People have always wanted to know the answers to questions like these. Some of the people of long ago thought that they could find the answers from astrologers, who "read" the stars. The people of ancient Greece went to oracles instead.

At an oracle there was a priest or a priestess who was supposed to be able to find out from the gods the answers to questions. At the oracle of Zeus, which was at Dodona in northern Greece, the priest listened to the oak trees round about. Zeus was supposed to speak to the priest by making the oak leaves rustle.

The most famous oracle was the oracle of Apollo at Delphi. It was often called the Delphic oracle. Here a priestess sat near a deep crack in the rocks. Vapor came from this crack. When she breathed the vapor, the priestess was supposed to hear Apollo's answers to questions. People came to this oracle not only from Greece but also from many other lands.

So many people came to the oracles that the priests and priestesses knew a great deal about what was going on in the world. Sometimes they gave wise answers that were easy to understand. But as a rule the answers were not very clear. Many people asked the oracle of Apollo to explain answers given them by the oracle of Zeus.

The priests and priestesses were very clever about giving answers that could be taken in more than one way. Suppose, for instance, a ruler was planning to go to war and asked the oracle whether he would win. The oracle might answer, "A great kingdom will be conquered." The ruler might think that the oracle meant that he would win. But if he lost and his kingdom was conquered, he could not blame the oracle. The sayings of an oracle were usually right, no matter what happened. (See CROESUS; MYTHS AND LEGENDS.)

Zeus
Supreme God

Oracle of Zeus

Delphic Oracle

A 17th Century Orchestra

**ORCHESTRA** Long ago, before the days of orchestras, men who liked to play on stringed instruments sometimes played together in groups called bands or consorts. Bands became popular. But music had not yet been written especially for instruments alone. The players therefore used music which had been written for singers.

The first real orchestra was organized in Italy in 1600 to play the music for an opera. The orchestra was hidden to make sure that the audience would watch the singers and not the players. The instruments in that orchestra were three flutes, a theorbo (lute with two necks), a lyre, a lute, and a harpsichord. The harpsichord

is a small instrument that looks like our grand piano of today.

After 1600 other instruments were added to orchestras. Composers also began to write special music for the orchestra. Franz Joseph Haydn, the "father of the symphony," started the practice of arranging players in different groups, or sections.

The modern symphony orchestra is made up of four sections, or groups, of players. The four sections are the stringed instruments, the wood-wind instruments, the brass instruments, and the percussion instruments. Most symphony orchestras have between 60 and 110 players. The string section is the most important section of the orchestra. The wood-wind instruments are next in importance. Then come the brasses, and, finally, the percussion instruments.

The usual seating plan for a symphony orchestra is given in the diagram. Conductors sometimes change this arrangement.

An orchestra always has a conductor. Long ago the conductor sat at a harpsichord. He played this instrument and directed the players at the same time. The conductor now stands in front of the players.

Today there are symphony orchestras in almost every large city in the world. In the

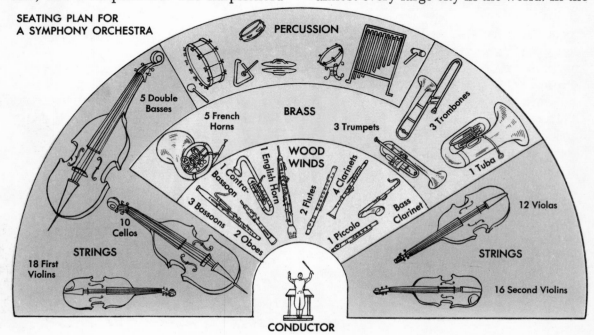

SEATING PLAN FOR
A SYMPHONY ORCHESTRA

PERCUSSION

5 Double Basses

5 French Horns

BRASS

3 Trumpets

3 Trombones

WOOD WINDS

1 English Horn

1 Contra-Bassoon

4 Clarinets

1 Tuba

3 Bassoons

2 Flutes

Bass Clarinet

2 Oboes

1 Piccolo

10 Cellos

12 Violas

STRINGS

STRINGS

18 First Violins

16 Second Violins

CONDUCTOR

United States some of the best are the orchestras of Boston, Chicago, New York, Philadelphia, and San Francisco.

A symphony orchestra of today usually has these instruments:

| Stringed Instruments | |
| --- | --- |
| 18 First violins | 8 to 10 Cellos |
| 16 Second violins | 5 to 8 Double basses |
| 12 Violas | 1 or 2 Harps |
| Wood Winds | |
| 1 or 2 Piccolos | 4 Clarinets |
| 2 to 4 Flutes | 1 Bass clarinet |
| 2 Oboes | 3 or 4 Bassoons |
| 1 English horn | 1 Contrabassoon |
| Brasses | |
| 3 to 5 French horns | 3 or more Trombones |
| 3 or 4 Trumpets | 1 Tuba |
| Percussion Instruments | |
| (usually played by two or three players) | |
| 2 or more Tympani | 1 Tambourine |
| 1 Snare drum | 1 Gong |
| 1 Bass drum | 1 Xylophone |
| 1 Pair of cymbals | 1 Set of bells |
| 1 Triangle | 1 Set of tubular chimes |
| 1 Pair of castanets | 1 Celesta |

**ORCHIDS** No flowers in flower shops are more beautiful than the orchids. And very few cut flowers last longer.

The natural home of most of the flower shop orchids is the hot, steamy jungle land near the equator. Many of these orchids grow perched on the branches of trees. Getting enough water is a problem for any perching plant. The roots of the perching orchids are spongy on the outside. The roots can therefore soak up quickly any rain that falls on them. The orchids also have the help of some other plants— thread-like fungi. The fungi soak up water and carry it into the orchid roots.

The orchids' fungi helpers also help new orchid plants get a start in life. The seeds of orchids are very tiny—too small to be seen without a microscope. The wind blows them about. To grow they must land where the right fungi are at hand to hold them in place and help them take in water.

Although many orchids grow perched on other plants, some grow in the ground. The moccasin flower and the showy lady's-slipper are ground-growing orchids. They are among the loveliest wild flowers in the

Spongy orchid roots soak up falling rain.

United States. Like perching orchids, ground-growing orchids have fungi helpers.

Today most flower-shop orchids are raised in hothouses. Orchid growers had to learn about the orchids' fungi helpers before they could raise these beautiful flowers. It takes from four to eight years for an orchid plant raised from seed to bloom.

One color is so common among hothouse orchids, it is called orchid. But orchids may be white, pink, yellow, green, or brown.

Only one kind of orchid produces anything valuable besides flowers. This is the vanilla orchid. The flavoring vanilla comes from it. (See EPIPHYTE; FUNGI.)

The lady's-slipper of North America is a member of the orchid family.

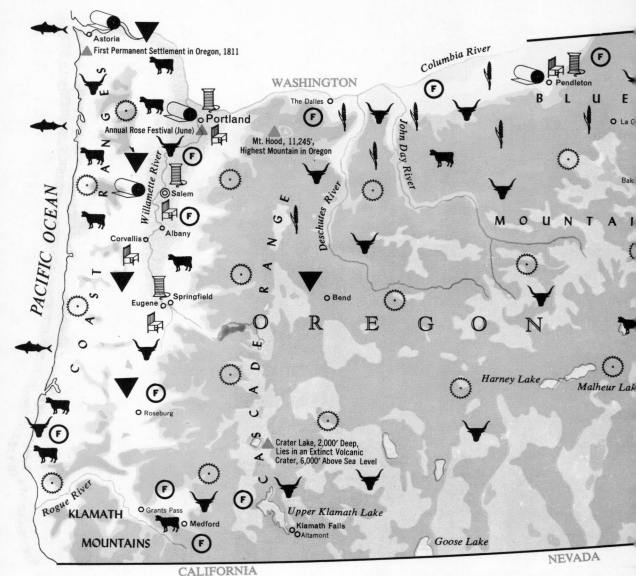

Astoria

First Permanent Settlement in Oregon, 1811

WASHINGTON

*Columbia River*

The Dalles

Pendleton

BLUE

La G

*John Day River*

Annual Rose Festival (June)

Portland

Mt. Hood, 11,245',
Highest Mountain in Oregon

MOUNTAI

Bak

C O A S T   R A N G E S

*Willamette River*

Salem

Albany

Corvallis

*Deschutes River*

C A S C A D E   R A N G E

O R E G O N

PACIFIC OCEAN

Eugene   Springfield

Bend

Harney Lake

Malheur Lak

Roseburg

Crater Lake, 2,000' Deep,
Lies in an Extinct Volcanic
Crater, 6,000' Above Sea Level

*Rogue River*

KLAMATH

Grants Pass

Medford

MOUNTAINS

*Upper Klamath Lake*

Klamath Falls
Altamont

Goose Lake

NEVADA

CALIFORNIA

Skiing

State Flower:
Oregon Grape

State
Seal

State Capitol

State Bird:
Western
Meadowlark

**OREGON** This region of the Pacific
Northwest became the state of Oregon only
a century ago—in 1859. Lewis and Clark
reached the Columbia River, which had
formerly been called the Oregon, in 1805.
It was from the original name of the river
that the state was named. The first settlement was made in 1811.

People first began to move into Oregon
in numbers during the 1840's and 1850's.
Thousands of American pioneers in covered wagons followed the Oregon Trail to
make their homes in this land of promise.
Some early pioneers braved the long sea

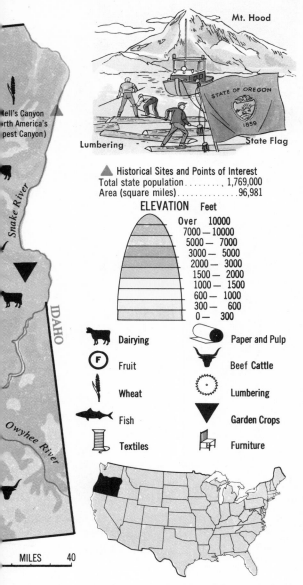

Lumbering    State Flag

▲ Historical Sites and Points of Interest
Total state population . . . . . . . . 1,769,000
Area (square miles) . . . . . . . . . . . . . 96,981

ELEVATION   Feet

Over   10000
7000 — 10000
5000 —  7000
3000 —  5000
2000 —  3000
1500 —  2000
1000 —  1500
 600 —  1000
 300 —   600
   0 —   300

Dairying             Paper and Pulp

Ⓕ Fruit              Beef Cattle

Wheat                Lumbering

Fish                 Garden Crops

Textiles             Furniture

MILES    40

and paper, plywood, and fiberboard are produced in large quantities. Lumbermen use good methods of cutting trees, planting tree "farms," and operating mills. They want to keep Oregon first in lumber.

Oregon's farms produce more food than is used in the state. Thousands of cars of fresh fruit and vegetables move out of the state each year. Salem, the capital city, is a fruit and vegetable processing center.

Most of the farms are in the fertile Willamette Valley. The winters there are mild, and the summers are rather cool. Most of the year's rain falls in the winter. Much land is used for raspberries and loganberries. There are many orchards of plums, cherries, pears, and apples. There are many dairy farms here where grass stays green throughout the year. Wheat is grown on other farms. Most of the valley farmers do not water their fields. New irrigation works will increase the crops from this area. Irrigation has boosted crops in dry eastern Oregon. East of the mountains are millions of acres of grazing lands.

People feared that the important salmon industry on the Columbia River would be ruined by the Bonneville Dam across the river. But fish "ladders" were built to let the salmon get past the dam. The salmon industry was saved. Columbia river salmon are caught both in the river and in the ocean. The main canneries are at Astoria.

Water is the key to many changes in Oregon. The big dams of the Columbia River system provide electric power for new factories. Among them are factories for processing uranium, wood pulp, frozen foods, and aluminum.

Portland, a city of almost 400,000, is the chief center of manufacturing and trade. It has a good location near the place where the Willamette River joins the Columbia. The valley of the Columbia is one of the few passageways through the mountains. Portland, the "City of Roses" is the "Gateway to Oregon" for air, rail, highway, or ocean travel.

voyage "round the Horn." The settlers found fertile soils, vast forests, fast-flowing streams, and beautiful mountains. The settlers made good use of these riches.

Later settlers came in trains and automobiles. It is still one of the less populous states. It has, however, more than four times as many people as it had 50 years ago. As in the past, there are many good ways for Oregonians to make a living.

The rain forests of western Oregon furnish the raw materials for the state's biggest business. The Douglas fir is the king of the trees in those forests. Lumber, pulp

Once the pipe organ was pumped by hand.

**ORGAN** Of all musical instruments pipe organs are the largest. Pipe organs may have hundreds or even thousands of pipes in them. One big organ in Philadelphia has 40,000. The pipes of a pipe organ are of many different shapes and sizes. One pipe may be as tall as a four-story building while another measures only a few inches. One may be a foot across while another is smaller around than your little finger. Each pipe gives out a certain note.

The ancestor of the pipe organ was a very simple little instrument called the pipes of Pan. The player blew across the ends of hollow reeds. Blowing across the ends of the reeds made the air inside them move, or vibrate, and produce a sound. No two pipes were of the same size and no two gave off the same sound.

Of course, the player does not blow across the openings of the big pipes of a pipe organ. Air comes instead from a big air chamber. Air is forced into this air chamber with a big bellows or with an electric fan. Before the days of electricity every pipe organ had to be worked with a bellows. One pipe organ used in England had to have 75 men to pump the bellows.

To play a pipe organ the player sends air into first one pipe or group of pipes and then into another. He does this by pushing down keys. On a pipe organ there are several rows of keys that an organist plays with his hands, just like the keys on a piano. The player plays one other row of keys, which are really pedals, with his feet. Perhaps the most unusual fact about pipe organs is that one note can be made to sound like many other orchestral instruments by pulling knobs called stops.

It takes a great deal of skill to play a pipe organ well. But no other instrument can produce music of such grandeur.

Pipe organs are not the only organs. There are also reed organs. They used to be very common in homes and small churches. Reed organs look somewhat like small pianos but sound very different. The player works a bellows with his feet. As he pushes the keys down, a valve releases some air against thin strips of material like the reed in a clarinet. These reeds move, or vibrate, and produce the sound.

Now there are electric organs, too. They are much like reed organs except that air is pumped by an electric motor instead of a bellows. They can be played much faster than an ordinary reed organ. Electric organs also have loud-speakers. (See BACH, JOHANN SEBASTIAN; MUSIC; PIANO; WIND INSTRUMENTS.)

Some pipe organs have two keyboards.

Fishing

Rice Fields

**OSAKA** The second-largest city in Japan is Osaka. It has over 2,500,000 people.

In some ways Osaka is much like Chicago, the second largest city in the United States. Osaka is a great railroad center. It is, moreover, the chief city in an important industrial district. In Osaka there are many mills and factories. Making heavy machinery, weaving cloth, and building ships are three of the kinds of work the people of Osaka do.

Osaka is also a port city. For a long time big boats could not reach it. Now the shallow harbor at the eastern end of Osaka Bay has been improved to take care of large ships. Kobe used to be the port for Osaka just as Yokohama is for Tokyo. Kobe and Osaka are just 16 miles apart. Most overseas passenger traffic to and from the region is still handled at Kobe.

Businessmen have helped make Osaka the commercial center of Japan. The central business district of Osaka has mostly western-type buildings. But much of the city is typically Japanese. Even the factories have a distinctly oriental look. In the shopping and amusement center there are colorful bazaars. There is one theater that has only puppet shows. (See JAPAN.)

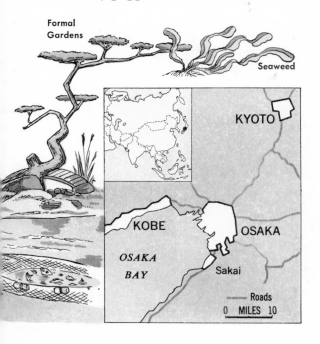

Ostriches protect themselves by kicking.

**OSTRICH** The ostrich is the largest of all the birds of today. A full-grown ostrich may weigh more than 200 pounds. This big bird is a native of southern Africa and western Asia. But there are very few wild ostriches left. Like all birds, ostriches have feathers, two legs, and two wings. But although they have wings they cannot fly. They use their wings as brakes or to help them turn as they run.

Ostriches are able to run very fast—from 40 to 60 miles per hour. They can easily outrun most of their enemies. Even a hunter on horseback cannot overtake one.

An ostrich egg weighs about three pounds—as much as two dozen chicken eggs. Baby ostriches are the size of full-grown chickens. It takes a baby ostrich at least three years to grow up.

Ostriches eat plant food—leaves, seeds, and fruits. They can go for days without water. For this reason the ostrich's nickname, "camel bird," is a good one. Besides, ostriches walk a little like camels.

These big birds have some very large feathers, or plumes. Ostrich plumes were once much used to trim hats. In the early 1900's ostrich farms were thriving in South Africa and the United States. Now ostrich feathers are out of fashion.

There is no ground for the idea that an ostrich buries its head in the sand when it is in danger. (See BIRDS.)

Sea Otter

River Otter

**OTTER** Nowhere in the world are there animals that are more fun to watch than a family of river otters. Young otters are very playful. One of their ways of playing is to slide down a mud slide into the water. In winter they slide down snowbanks instead.

Otters are excellent animals for a zoo, for they always put on a show for visitors. They turn somersaults, have swimming races, and throw themselves down their slides both forwards and backwards. An otter in one zoo always balanced a little rock on its nose when it went swimming. It always used the same rock. In between swims the otter hid the rock in a crack.

Sea otters are larger than river otters. They seldom come on land. Often they float on their backs and use their chests as dining tables. As they float on their backs, they often play with shells and seaweed.

Otters are cousins of the weasels, the minks, and the skunks. They eat fish and other small animals. Otters are excellent swimmers and divers. They are very well fitted for living in water. Their feet are webbed. Their tails are good rudders. They can close both their ears and their noses when they are under water. Their heavy fur protects them when the water is cold. Besides, they have a layer of fat under their skin that helps keep them warm.

Otters are so much at home in the water that people used to think they were half fish. Because of the idea that otters were part fish, the Roman Catholic Church during the Middle Ages permitted otter meat to be eaten on days of fasting.

Far too many otters have been killed for their beautiful fur. Now they are being protected. (See FURS; SKUNK; ZOOS.)

**OWLS** These birds have the reputation of being very wise. Owls look wise because of their big eyes. Really, owls are not any more intelligent than many other birds.

There are dozens of kinds of owls. Some are much bigger than others. The elf owl is one of the smallest. It lives in the southwestern United States. Its nests are in old woodpecker holes in giant cactus plants. It is only six inches high. The great gray owl, on the other hand, is nearly a yard tall. The great gray owl is the biggest owl in North America. Under normal conditions it lives in Canada, but it comes down to visit the United States when food farther north is scarce.

All owls are birds of prey. They swallow whole the small animals they catch. They help the farmers by catching field mice. Owls do their hunting at night. Their big eyes help them see in dim light.

The screech owl is either gray or reddish brown.

The barn owl has a white, heart-shaped face.

Some owls look as if they had big ears as well as big eyes. But their big "ears" are only tufts of feathers. All owls have ears, but their real ears are hidden under their feathers.

Some owls get their names from the sounds they make. The screech owls and the hoot owls do. The barred owl, so-called because of its bars of different-colored feathers, is one of the hoot owls. There is no more lonesome sound in the woods at night than the "hoo-hoo-hoo-hoo-hoo-hoo-hoo-hooah" of a barred owl. (See BIRDS.)

The "horns" of the horned owl are feathers.

**OXYGEN** No one can live for more than a very few minutes without oxygen. We have to have water and food, too, but we can go without them longer.

We get oxygen from the air we breathe. For oxygen is one of the gases in the air. About one-fifth of the air is oxygen.

By looking at the air no one can tell how much oxygen there is in it. Oxygen is invisible just as all the gases in the air are. A bottle full of oxygen looks empty.

Oxygen is a gas, but it is a part of many substances that are not gases. It is one of the elements that make up all the other substances in the world. Oxygen is in many of the chemicals scientists work with. It is in many of the common things around us, too. It is in butter and sugar and water. It is in cotton and chewing gum and chalk. It is also in most of the rocks that the earth's crust is made of.

The list of things that contain oxygen could be made very long. Even we ourselves are part oxygen. So are all other animals and all plants.

All animals have to breathe in oxygen just as we do. All the animals in the world use up a great deal of oxygen. Fires use up oxygen when they burn. All the fires in the world use up a great deal. Why hasn't all the oxygen in the air been used up? It would have been if it were not for green plants. During the daytime they throw away oxygen. They have it left over from the substances from which they make their food. At night green plants use up oxygen just as we do. But they throw away more in the daytime than they use up at night. Because of green plants, the amount of oxygen in the air stays about the same year in and year out.

High above the earth the air is thin. A person cannot get all the oxygen he needs by breathing this air. When flying high in this thin air pilots may carry tanks of oxygen with them. Sick people sometimes need extra oxygen. Fortunately, scientists have found out how to get oxygen from the air and from some of the many substances in which oxygen is hidden.

Oxygen can be changed to a liquid. Rockets meant to go high above the earth carry tanks of liquid oxygen along with their fuel. (See AIR; BREATHING; ELEMENTS; LIQUID AIR; ROCKETS.)

**OYSTERS** Along the world's seashores there are thousands and thousands of kinds of animals with shells. Among them are the oysters. Far back in the days before written history, people found out that some oysters are good to eat. Ancient people left behind great piles of oyster shells that tell the story. Oysters are still one of our favorite foods. Besides, most true pearls come from oysters.

There are at least 100 kinds of oysters. Some grow to be only an inch or so long. But there are giants that grow nearly a yard long. Most of those we buy measure four or five inches across their shells.

An oyster's "house" is made up of two shells. A hinge at one end fastens them together. With its strong muscle an oyster can open and close its shells.

The oysters we eat live in temperate shallow water. A grown-up oyster stays fastened to a rock or something else hard. Most of the time it holds its shells partly open. Water flows in and out, bringing oxygen and food and carrying wastes away.

These animals of the seashore make such good eating not only for us but for other animals that they probably would have disappeared long ago if they did not lay so many eggs. One oyster may lay more than 50 million in a single season.

When first hatched, oysters have no shells. The baby oysters are about the size of a pin point. When they are a day old their shells have begun to form. The baby oysters swim about freely for two weeks or so. Then they fasten themselves to something solid. They stay fastened to the same spot for the rest of their lives.

Some people do oyster "farming." They help to protect the oysters on their farms, which, of course, are under water, from the oyster drill, the starfish, and other oyster enemies. Oyster farmers make sure that there will be rocks or shells for the young oysters that hatch to fasten themselves to.

Not many pearls come from the kinds of oysters we eat. Most pearls come from pearl oysters which live in warm seas. (See MOLLUSKS; PEARLS; SHELLFISH.)

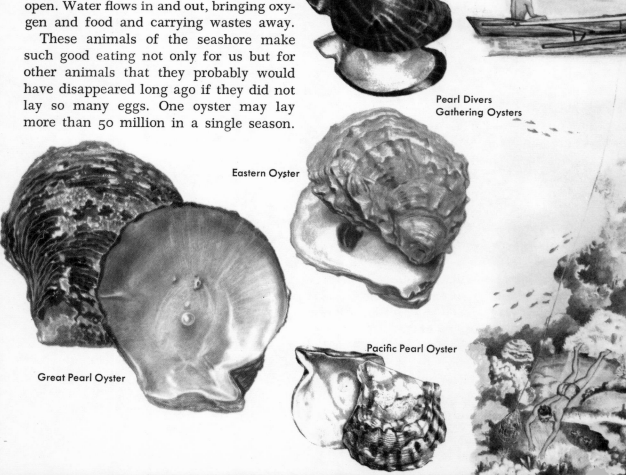

Atlantic Wing Oyster

Pearl Divers Gathering Oysters

Eastern Oyster

Great Pearl Oyster

Pacific Pearl Oyster

The letter *P* can be traced back to this letter in the Phoenician alphabet: ʔ . In the beginning the letter was probably a picture, perhaps the picture of a mouth. But by the time it reached the Phoenicians it did not look much like the picture of anything. The Greeks wrote it first one way ( Γ ) and then another ( Π ). The Romans changed it to look like this: P. It came down from them unchanged.

*P* stands for only one sound—the sound it has in *puppy* and *play*. But in some words it is silent. *Raspberry, cupboard,* and *psalm* are three of them.

**PACIFIC OCEAN** The Pacific Ocean is the world's biggest ocean. It is bigger than all the continents put together. This great ocean stretches from the Americas nearly halfway round the earth to Asia and Australia. One can turn a globe so that almost nothing but the Pacific shows.

The Pacific gets its name because it is usually calm. "Pacific" means "peaceful" or "calm." But this ocean is not always calm. Great windstorms called typhoons sometimes sweep over it. They are much like the hurricanes of the Atlantic but often are even more violent.

There are mountains near the coasts of most of the lands around the Pacific. Many of the mountains are volcanoes. These volcanoes are sometimes called the Pacific's "rim of fire."

There are thousands of islands in the Pacific. Many of them are the tops of volcanoes. New volcanic islands appear from time to time. Many of the islands of the Pacific have been made bigger by corals. Almost every island in the South Pacific has a rim of coral around it.

Life is easy for the natives on many South Pacific islands. The weather is warm. Houses and clothing can be simple since they do not have to protect people from the cold. Coconut palms and breadfruit trees furnish food. There are countless fish in the sea for them to catch.

The Pacific is a busy highway, although it is not as busy as the Atlantic. Ships crossing the Pacific follow shipping lanes. There are parts of this big ocean that ships never reach. Except at the Far North, a journey across the Pacific is much longer than a journey across the Atlantic. Planes that make the long trip across have to stop for fuel on the way. Fortunately there are islands that make good stepping stones.

The Pacific is deep as well as wide. The deepest place found so far is near the Marianas Islands. There the ocean is 35,948 feet deep—between six and seven miles.

Some scientists have suggested a strange explanation of the great size of the Pacific. They say that perhaps the earth, as it whirled around back in the time when it was not yet solid, threw off a big chunk of itself. This chunk became the moon. The hole it left became the bed of the Pacific. This idea is not widely held. But knowing about it helps us remember how big and deep the Pacific is. (See ATLANTIC OCEAN; BALBOA, VASCO NÚÑEZ DE; HAWAII; OCEANS; VOLCANOES.)

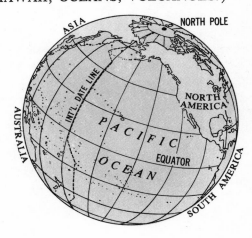

Pagodas are several-storied temples and shrines.

**PAGODA** At a glance it is easy to see that the picture above is a picture of some place in the Far East. For there are two pagodas in the picture and pagodas are not normally found anywhere else.

Pagodas are towers made up of several stories. A pagoda always has an odd number of stories. The builders think that odd numbers are lucky.

Most pagodas are temples or parts of temples. The idea of pagodas spread from India to other parts of Asia along with the religion called Buddhism.

The Chinese, as they built pagodas, changed the shape somewhat. It is the Chinese pagoda, which the Japanese copied, that most people know best. A Chinese pagoda has eight sides. Wide eaves that turn up at the corners reach out above each story. Small bells are often hung from the eaves so that they will tinkle when the wind blows. Chinese pagodas are built of brick, glazed tile, or porcelain. Most Japanese pagodas are wooden.

Many pagodas are decorated with gold. The world's tallest pagoda stands on a hill near the heart of the city of Rangoon, the capital of Burma. It is the Shwe Dagon Pagoda. Every inch of the walls of this 326-foot tall pagoda is covered with pure gold. (See BUDDHA.)

**PAINT** The first paint we know about was used by cave men more than 10,000 years ago. The cave men painted colored pictures on the walls of some of their caves.

Their paint was made of coloring matter, or pigments, held together with a binder. The pigments were mostly ochers (O kers). Ochers are minerals made of iron and oxygen. They are red, yellow, orange, or brown in color. These are the colors the cave men used most. They also used black. Their black pigment probably came from burned bones. The binder in their paint was grease or oil from animals they killed.

We know about the paint of the cave men because some of the cave pictures have lasted till today. Besides, flat stones have been found on which the pigments were ground. Shells and hollow bones in which the pigments were stored have also been found. The pictures of the cave men were probably prayers for good hunting. The colors were used to make the pictures more beautiful.

Paint is still much used for pictures and for other decorations. But it serves another purpose, too. It is used to make materials last longer. A steel bridge like the one across the Golden Gate would soon rust away if paint did not protect it from air and moisture. The wood of a wooden building exposed to the weather would decay. Paint is used in enormous amounts. In the United States alone paint factories make about half a billion gallons a year.

Cave men painted hunting scenes on cave walls.

Today's paints are made mostly of pigments, binders, and thinners. The pigments and binders form the paint film that is left when the paint dries. The thinners make the paint easy to spread. They evaporate. Other materials may be added to make paints suitable for special purposes. Many paints, for instance, have in them a drier that makes them dry fast.

Every paint maker has his own recipe for paint. Many modern paints are rather complicated mixtures. A few of the kinds of paint used today are listed below.

### PAINTS USED BY ARTISTS

*Water color*—This paint is thinned with water for spreading. It is used for painting on paper. It is transparent.

*Poster paint*—This paint is also thinned with water, but it is thicker than water color and is not transparent. It is used for painting on paper. It is sometimes called tempera.

*Casein paint*—The pigments are made from casein, which comes from milk. They can be used for painting on canvas, wood, paper, or glass. These pigments, too, are mixed with water.

*Oil paint*—The pigments are mixed with oil. It is used chiefly for painting pictures on canvas.

### PAINTS USED FOR OTHER PURPOSES

*House paint*—The pigments are mixed with oil. House paints are made to last a long time.

*Wall paint*—The pigments are mixed with many different binders and thinners. Some, like calcimine, are thinned with water. Some contain rubber; some contain casein. Some have in them varnish that gives them a glossy finish. Varnish is made from resins, mostly from trees. Wall paints are used chiefly on plaster and wood.

*Enamel*—Enough varnish is added to give a very hard, glossy finish. Enamels are used on wood and metal.

*Lacquer*—Lacquers contain either natural or artificial varnishes. They are quick-drying. The paints used for automobiles are lacquers.

*Wood stains*—Wood alcohol or some similar thinner is used. Wood stains are only for bare wood. Their finish is dull. They do not cover well.

*Luminous paints*—These paints contain radium or something similar that makes them glow in the dark.

Many pigments are available to paint makers today. Some are called natural pigments. These include ochers and other minerals much like them. But scientists have learned to make many, many more. One pigment people learned to make more than 2,000 years ago is white lead. It has been used in paint ever since. It is good because it covers up well what is under it. Now titanium dioxide, another pigment, is taking the place of white lead. This new pigment is an even better coverer, is a purer white, and lasts longer.

As long ago as the time of the ancient Egyptians linseed oil was being used as a binder. Linseed oil comes from the seeds of the flax plant, the same plant that gives us the fibers for linen. Linseed oil is still much used, but paint makers in recent times have developed many other materials that make good binders.

Turpentine, which comes from pine trees, is a thinner that has been used for a long time and is still used. Today there are many other good thinners. Some of them are made from coal tar or petroleum.

A great deal of experimenting is now being done with paints. In the paint factories of the United States more than 2,000 scientists plan and try out ways of making paints better. We can expect the paints of tomorrow to be even more beautiful, easier to use, and longer lasting than the paints of today. (See CAVE MAN; COAL TAR; DYES; FLAX; PAINTERS AND PAINTING; TURPENTINE.)

**PAINTED DESERT** In Arizona, not far from the marvelous Grand Canyon, there is a great level stretch of land called the Painted Desert. It gets the "painted" in its name from the colors in its rocks. They are mostly red.

The Painted Desert is a part of the Colorado Plateau. It is several thousand feet above sea level. But its rocks tell that it has not always been above sea level. The rocks are mostly sandstone and shale, many layers of which were formed under ancient seas. The region was pushed up high above sea level only about a million years ago.

In time the Painted Desert will not be the great level stretch of land it is now. Streams will wear their way down into it, making deep canyons. Finally it will be cut up into mountains like those that rise from the floor of the Grand Canyon.

"The Last Supper" by Leonardo da Vinci

Early Cave-man Painting

Egyptian Wall Painting

Mural by Diego Rivera

**PAINTERS AND PAINTING** "The Last Supper" is one of the world's most famous paintings. It is on one wall of a dark dining hall of a church in Milan, Italy. Leonardo da Vinci painted "The Last Supper." The picture shows Jesus eating for the last time with his 12 disciples. In the 450 years since the picture was painted, it has faded and part of the paint has cracked off.

This famous painting might be still as beautiful as when it was first painted if Leonardo had not been an experimenter. It is not surprising that the picture was painted on a wall. Most of the pictures of that time and of earlier times were painted on walls. Many murals—pictures on walls —are still painted today. The Mexican artist Diego Rivera, for instance, was a famous mural painter of recent times. But it is surprising that Leonardo used the kind of paint that he did. For 3,000 years most wall paintings had been frescoes. In fresco painting, the painting is done on wet plaster with colors that soak into the wet plaster. The painter must paint fast before the plaster dries. Frescoes last very well. Some are far older than "The Last Supper," and are still in good condition.

But Leonardo decided to experiment with painting in tempera on a specially prepared wall. In tempera painting the colors are mixed with egg and glue. The artist does not have to hurry; he can paint slowly. Tempera works well on a dry wall. But the wall on which "The Last Supper" was painted was not really dry. The climate of Milan is very damp. The dampness made the wall so moist that the painting molded and was almost ruined.

Painting has been important since the days of the cave men. In their caves are beautiful pictures of animals. These pictures cannot have been just for decoration. As a rule they are deep inside the caves where they are very hard to see. They must have had something to do with hunting. Perhaps the painters were trying to work magic to attract the animals. Perhaps the pictures were prayers for good hunting.

Egyptian painting began as a decoration on their stone carvings. But by 3,500 years ago they had begun painting pictures on flat walls—the walls of their tombs and palaces. There was no perspective or shading in their pictures. But some of their pictures are very decorative.

The first true frescoes, as far as anyone knows, were painted by the people of ancient Crete. The frescoes were on the walls of their palaces.

The Greeks painted on their sculpture. They also painted pictures on walls, but none of their pictures has lasted.

During the Dark Ages the monks did the most to keep art alive in Europe. A great deal of their painting was done in books. In those days all books had to be copied by hand. The monks did most of the copying. They decorated some of the books they copied with wonderful designs and pictures. They used lovely colors and much gold. The books they decorated are called illuminated manuscripts.

We know much more about early painting than about early painters. No one knows the names of the cave men who painted the pictures in the caves. We do not know of any famous painters in Egypt or in Crete. A few names of Greek painters have come down to us, but we know very little about their work. We know of no famous Roman painters. But the story changed some 650 years ago when the Renaissance began. A revival of art began in Italy and spread to other countries.

During the Renaissance there were more great artists than the world had ever had before or has ever had at one time since. Pictures were in such demand that many artists could earn a good living by painting. Rulers kept painters at their courts.

The painters of the Renaissance tried to make things look real. Some were noted for beautiful line, some for form, some for perspective. The painters of Venice became noted for their vivid colors.

Great painting did not end with the Renaissance. There have been many great painters since. Some of these artists have painted in fresco and tempera. Some have used water colors or oils.

Water-color paint is usually transparent. The paper on which it is done shows through the paint. A water-color picture must be painted very quickly so that the paint will not dry before the picture is finished. Water color is one of the most difficult kinds of paint to handle. If a water-color picture still looks wet after it is dry, it is considered especially good.

Oil painting is one of the easiest kinds of painting. As anyone would guess, oil paint gets its name because the colors are mixed with oil. Oil paint dries slowly. If a painter makes a mistake, he can scrape off the paint and try again. Many of the old masters put many coats of varnish on their finished oil paintings. The pictures are as beautiful today as they were long ago.

In the past six centuries many artists have chosen to paint pictures to hang on walls rather than to paint on the walls themselves. Pictures made to hang on walls are often called easel pictures.

Painters have worked out many ways of painting. Some painting is done with free brush strokes. When you look at the picture you can see where the brush stroke started and where it ended. Sometimes an artist dips his brush first in blue and then in green. The result is a stroke that is part green and part blue. Some artists paint by putting the color on the canvas in tiny dots. Some make little wiggly lines. Some put on the paint so that the surface is very smooth. Others make the surface very rough; they put on oil paint with a palette knife instead of a brush. The paint stands out in little humps all over the picture.

Some paintings are realistic. Others, called abstract paintings, are painted like designs. Some show much imagination. Others are more like photographs. Some are mostly for decoration. Others have a message for those who see them. Some paintings tell a story. They may stir up feelings of gladness or gloom or wonder. Paintings showing scenes from everyday life are called "genre" (JOHN er) paintings.

Listing all the famous painters would take many, many pages. The chart on the next two pages lists some of the most famous. (See GIOTTO; MICHELANGELO; MODERN ART; RAPHAEL; REMBRANDT; RENAISSANCE; RENOIR; VINCI, LEONARDO DA.)

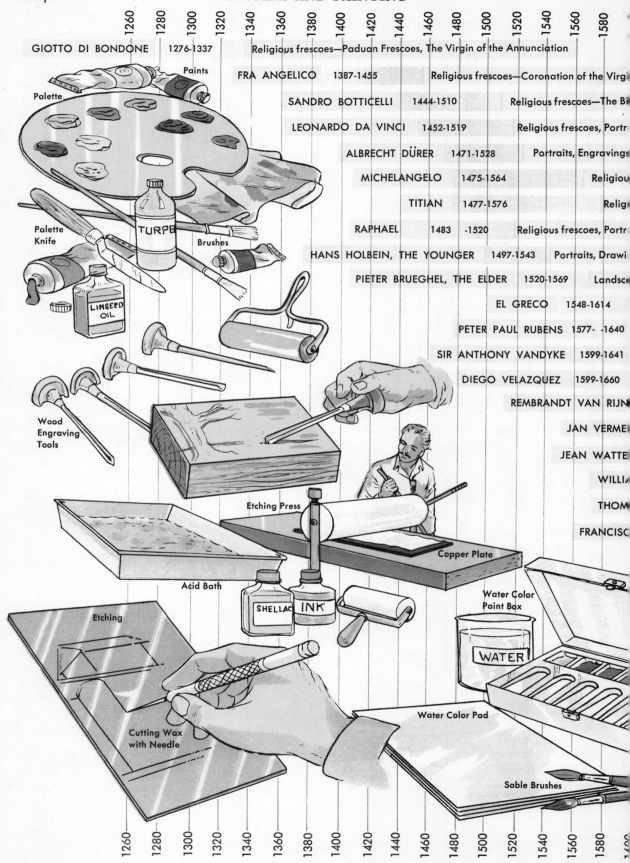

| | 1260 | 1280 | 1300 | 1320 | 1340 | 1360 | 1380 | 1400 | 1420 | 1440 | 1460 | 1480 | 1500 | 1520 | 1540 | 1560 | 1580 |
|---|---|---|---|---|---|---|---|---|---|---|---|---|---|---|---|---|---|

GIOTTO DI BONDONE    1276-1337    Religious frescoes—Paduan Frescoes, The Virgin of the Annunciation

FRA ANGELICO    1387-1455    Religious frescoes—Coronation of the Virgi

SANDRO BOTTICELLI    1444-1510    Religious frescoes—The Bi

LEONARDO DA VINCI    1452-1519    Religious frescoes, Portr

ALBRECHT DÜRER    1471-1528    Portraits, Engravings

MICHELANGELO    1475-1564    Religiou

TITIAN    1477-1576    Relig

RAPHAEL    1483    -1520    Religious frescoes, Portr

HANS HOLBEIN, THE YOUNGER    1497-1543    Portraits, Drawi

PIETER BRUEGHEL, THE ELDER    1520-1569    Landsc

EL GRECO    1548-1614

PETER PAUL RUBENS    1577- -1640

SIR ANTHONY VANDYKE    1599-1641

DIEGO VELAZQUEZ    1599-1660

REMBRANDT VAN RIJN

JAN VERME

JEAN WATTE

WILLI

THOM

FRANCISC

Paints

Palette

Palette Knife

TURPE

Brushes

LINSEED OIL

Wood Engraving Tools

Etching Press

Copper Plate

Acid Bath

SHELLAC    INK

Water Color Paint Box

Etching

WATER

Water Color Pad

Cutting Wax with Needle

Sable Brushes

| | 1260 | 1280 | 1300 | 1320 | 1340 | 1360 | 1380 | 1400 | 1420 | 1440 | 1460 | 1480 | 1500 | 1520 | 1540 | 1560 | 1580 |
|---|---|---|---|---|---|---|---|---|---|---|---|---|---|---|---|---|---|

1660 1680 1700 1720 1740 1760 1780 1800 1820 1840 1860 1880 1900 1920 1940 1960

**Engraving**

**Etching**

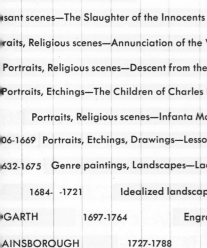

**Wood Cut**

**Water Color**

**Oil**

esco at Orvieto

Venus

Last Supper, Madonna of the Rocks

trait of Lucas Baumgärtner, The Apostles

scoes—The Last Judgment

scoes, Portraits—Venus and the Lute Player

ine Madonna

odcuts—Portrait of Erasmus

sant scenes—The Slaughter of the Innocents

aits, Religious scenes—Annunciation of the Virgin, View of Toledo, Burial of Count Orgaz

Portraits, Religious scenes—Descent from the Cross

Portraits, Etchings—The Children of Charles I

Portraits, Religious scenes—Infanta Maria Theresa, Don Baltazar Carlos

06-1669  Portraits, Etchings, Drawings—Lesson in Anatomy, Syndics of the Cloth Hall

632-1675  Genre paintings, Landscapes—Lady at a Casement, Girl with Flute

1684- -1721  Idealized landscapes—Embarkation for Cythera

GARTH  1697-1764  Engravings, Portraits—The Rake's Progress, Shrimp Girl

AINSBOROUGH  1727-1788  Portraits, Landscapes—The Blue Boy

GOYA Y LUCIENTES  1746-1828  Etchings, Portraits, Frescoes—The Shooting, Disasters of the War

JOSEPH M. W. TURNER  1775-1851  Landscapes, Drawings—The Slave Ship at Dawn

JEAN BAPTISTE COROT  1796-1875  Landscapes, Portraits—Dance of the Nymphs

JEAN FRANCOIS MILLET  1814-1875  Peasant scenes—Bringing Home the Newborn Calf

JAMES MC NEILL WHISTLER  1834-1903  Etchings, Portraits—Southampton Water

PAUL CÉZANNE  1839-1906  Landscapes, Still lifes—L'Estaque

CLAUDE MONET  1840-1926  Landscapes—Argenteuil on-the-Seine

PIERRE AUGUSTE RENOIR  1841-1919  Portraits, Landscapes—On the Terrace

HENRI ROUSSEAU  1844-1910  Jungle scenes—The Girl in the Wood

VINCENT VAN GOGH  1853- -1890  Landscapes, Portraits, Still lites—Sunflowers

HENRI MATISSE  1869-1954  Indoor scenes—The Red Studio

PABLO PICASSO  1881-  Abstract paintings, Portraits

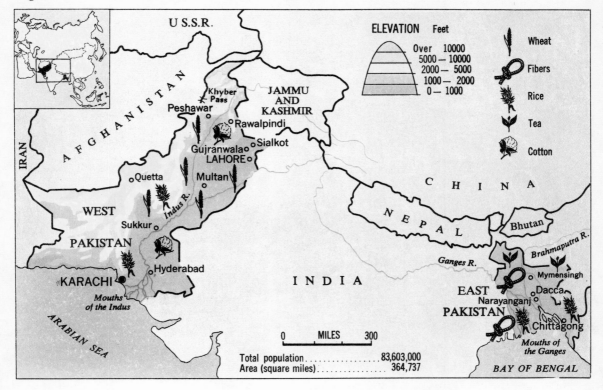

ELEVATION Feet

Over 10000
5000 — 10000
2000 — 5000
1000 — 2000
0 — 1000

Wheat

Fibers

Rice

Tea

Cotton

Total population .................. 83,603,000
Area (square miles) ............... 364,737

**PAKISTAN** This country of Asia is new. Books written before 1947 do not mention it. Maps made before that year do not show it. But it is not a newly discovered land. Four thousand years ago one of the earliest civilizations had grown up in the valley of the Indus River. There were cities with fine mud-brick houses, sewers, and water pipes. The people made beautiful pottery and jewelry. They could write, and they were the first people to weave cotton into cloth. But Pakistan was not a country until after World War II. In 1947 it was carved out of India.

For a long time before 1947 differences in religion had caused much trouble in India. Millions of the people of India were Moslems, or Mohammedans. Even more millions were Hindus. The Moslems wished to have a country of their own. After World War II this was brought about. The Moslems formed the Republic of Pakistan. "Pakistan" means "land of the pure." The Republic of Pakistan is a member of the British Commonwealth of Nations.

Pakistan looks strange on a map, for it is in two "pieces." Its western and eastern pieces are 920 miles apart. To get from one to the other, a person must travel across India, or make a boat trip of about 2,650 miles around southern India. Pakistan's capital is Karachi, a big seaport in West Pakistan. It has one of Asia's greatest airports, too, and is called Pakistan's "window to the world." A famous mountain pass—Khyber Pass—leads from northern West Pakistan to Afghanistan.

Most of Pakistan's millions of people are farmers and herdsmen. Though East Pakistan is smaller than West Pakistan, it has more people. Almost all of East Pakistan is low, hot, and rainy. It is green with crops the year round. The chief crops are rice and jute. But West Pakistan is green-brown and brown with much very dry land, and green in big stretches of irrigated crop land. Its chief crops are wheat and cotton. Pakistan is among the world's leading countries in producing jute, rice, cattle, cotton, and wheat.

At first many people feared that this new country could not hold its own. But it has done surprisingly well. It produces food for its millions of people and much jute and cotton to sell to other lands. It sells tea, wool, hides, and wheat, too. At first, it had to buy from other lands almost all the manufactured things it needed. But now many new factories are being started there, especially in northern West Pakistan. These factories are giving work to many people. They will help to make Pakistan prosperous. (See HINDU; INDIA; ISLAM; MOHAMMED.)

**PALEONTOLOGY** The science of paleontology is the study of the life of past ages. "Paleontology" comes from the Greek words meaning "old" and "knowledge." Scientists find out about the plants and animals of long ago by studying fossils. Fossils are traces found in rocks of ancient living things. (See BIRDS OF YESTERDAY; DINOSAURS; EARTH HISTORY; FOSSILS; LIFE THROUGH THE AGES; MAMMALS OF YESTERDAY.)

**PANAMA CANAL** Before 1914 the shortest way of sailing from the Atlantic Ocean to the Pacific Ocean was to go around the tip of South America. In 1914 a short cut became possible—the Panama Canal.

The Panama Canal crosses the Isthmus of Panama, the narrow neck of land that joins North and South America. The canal cuts the two continents apart.

For many years people had had the idea of this short cut. In 1880 a French engineer started a canal across the isthmus. He worked for seven years and spent millions of dollars but he did not build a canal. He was hindered partly by yellow fever, which killed many of his workmen.

In 1904 the United States Government took over the plan. Scientists had now found out that yellow fever is carried by mosquitoes. Building a canal meant partly fighting mosquitoes. Dr. William Gorgas was given the task of guarding the workers from yellow fever. He did his work well.

Of course mosquitoes were not the only problem. Digging a canal 40 miles long anywhere is not easy. Here the land was not level. Some of it was more than 300 feet above sea level. In some places the canal had to be cut through solid rock.

The engineers decided not to try to cut the canal down to sea level all the way. Even so, they had to blast out and shovel away more than 200,000,000 tons of rock and soil. Time after time there were landslides, and work had to be done all over again. Once an earthquake spoiled the work of many months. But at last the world's biggest "ditch" was dug.

Since the canal was not dug down to sea level all the way, locks had to be built in it. The locks make "steps" by which the ships can climb up to the highest point in the canal and then climb down again.

The canal was opened on October 10, 1913. On that day the president of the United States pushed a button that sent water pouring into it. The first ship passed through the canal on August 15, 1914.

Callao is a big seaport in Peru. It helps us to understand how important the Panama Canal is to know that the canal makes the journey by sea from Callao to New York 6,500 miles shorter than it was before.

Thousands of ships and millions of tons of goods go through this great canal every year. It is certainly one of the most important canals in the world. (See CANALS.)

Panama Canal Showing Ships in Locks

## EARLY CHINESE PAPERMAKING

Wasp and Paper Nest

Making Pulp

Closely-woven Cloth on Bamboo Frame

Dipping Frame Into Pulp

Drying Paper in the Sun

Piece of Oldest Known Paper

Chinese Paper Products

**PAPER** People knew how to write long before they had any paper. For thousands of years they wrote on such things as bark, bricks of soft clay, skins of animals, and pieces of broken pottery.

People might have had paper much earlier than they did if they had watched the paper wasps. These wasps make their nests of paper. To make the paper they first chew wood into a pulp. Then they spread the pulp out in a thin layer to dry. Much paper is now made of wood, but no one found out how to make paper of wood until long after paper was first made.

The first paper was made in China about 1,800 years ago. The Chinese may have got the idea by accident. The women of China often washed their clothes in pools. When they rubbed the clothes, they rubbed off little threads, or fibers. Perhaps some of these fibers were washed up on a rock and were dried by the sun to form a thin sheet. At least the Chinese found that they could make paper from cotton or linen rags. They found, too, that they could use fibers from the bark of the mulberry tree.

Of course the first paper was made by hand. The rags or pieces of bark were cut up into tiny pieces. They were then soaked and pounded into a pulp. For the next step a mold was needed. The mold was a screen with a frame around it. A layer of pulp was spread over the bottom of the mold. The mold was shaken about to make the fibers mat together. Some of the water from the pulp dripped through the holes in the screen. When the fibers had formed a sheet, the sheet was dried. Sometimes a press was used to squeeze out the water.

The Chinese kept paper a secret for hundreds of years. In 704 Arabs captured the Chinese city of Samarkand. They found a paper factory there. The Arabs spread papermaking across Africa into Europe. When printing was invented about 500 years ago, paper was waiting.

In 1799 Louis Robert, a Frenchman, invented a papermaking machine. It could make only a narrow ribbon of paper. Now a machine can make in five minutes a strip of paper 20 feet wide and a mile long. Today only the finest paper is handmade.

The best paper is still made of rags, but most paper is now made from the wood of spruce or pine trees. One papermaking machine can use the timber from several thousand acres in a year.

There are many steps in making wood into paper. After the logs reach the mill, the bark is taken off. The wood is then cut into chips. These are cooked with a chemical until the wood fibers separate. The fibers, or pulp, are washed and bleached. Any materials needed for the kind of paper being made are added.

In the papermaking machine, the wet pulp is formed into a sheet on a bronze screen. This sheet goes between rollers that squeeze out some moisture. The sheet is then dried as it passes over a series of heated rollers. The finished paper is wound on a big roll.

There are hundreds of kinds of paper. Some is thin; some is thick. Some paper is rough; some paper is smooth. Some can be torn easily; some is very tough.

The United States uses more than half the paper made in the world. The amount used in a single year averages more than 400 pounds a person. How our lives would change if for some reason we had to give up paper! (See LUMBERING; WOOD.)

**EARLY TO MODERN PAPERMAKING**

Paper Press

Rocks

Placing Damp Sheets on Boards For Drying

Lumber Going to the Paper Mill

Modern Soaking and Beating of Wood Pulp

DAILY RECORD

Uses of Paper

Cutaway Diagram of a Modern Papermaking Machine

Bronze Screen

Squeezing Rollers

Heated Drying Rollers

Roll of Finished Paper

**PAPYRUS** Much of the writing done in ancient Egypt and other countries of long ago was done on papyrus. The word "papyrus" is much like the word "paper." Papyrus was somewhat like paper.

Papyrus was made from the stems of the papyrus plant. The plant once grew in great masses along the Nile River in Egypt. Some of it can still be found there.

A papyrus plant has soft pith inside its stems. The best papyrus was made from only the pith. The pith was cut into strips and the strips were laid in two layers. In one of the layers the strips ran up and down. In the other they ran crosswise. Some kind of sticky material—no one is sure what—held the strips together.

The papyrus maker rolled the layers of pith together just as a cook rolls out piecrust. He then let the sheet of papyrus dry. After that he polished it with a smooth shell or a piece of bone or ivory.

Papyrus was made into books, but not into books like ours. Instead, the pages, or sheets, of papyrus were pasted together to form a long strip. One end of the strip was fastened to a rod of wood or ivory. The strip of papyrus was wound up around it. Usually the other end of the strip was also fastened to a rod.

Many papyrus books were only a few feet long. But some were much longer. Some of the papyrus books found in Egypt are over 150 feet long! (See EGYPT.)

**PARACHUTE** Airplanes are streamlined. They can push the air out of the way easily as they move through it. Being streamlined helps them move fast. Parachutes are just the opposite of streamlined. They are built to move through the air slowly.

A parachute is like a big umbrella. As a rule it is about 24 feet across. It spreads out so far that it cannot push the air out of its way easily. The air, as scientists say, offers great resistance.

Parachutes are much used in connection with airplanes. A flyer whose plane is in trouble may jump from it and float safely down to earth with his parachute. In war, parachutes help soldiers get to places hard to reach by land or sea. Soldiers trained to land by parachute are called paratroopers. Parachutes are a help, both in wartime and peacetime, in dropping supplies to people who are trapped in some way. They can carry supplies to fire fighters in forests. They are much used in bringing back to earth weather instruments and other scientific instruments sent high into the air by balloons. Jet planes sometimes use parachutes as brakes to help in landing.

Of course, an airman cannot have a parachute spread out over him when he is in his plane. The parachute must be folded up. But it must be arranged so that it can be opened easily. The flyer's parachute is fastened to a harness he wears. Some parachutes open automatically. But in many cases the flyer must open his parachute himself. When the flyer jumps from his plane, he lets himself fall until he is sure he is clear of the plane. Then he pulls a little cord attached to the parachute. This cord pulls open a small pilot parachute. This pilot parachute in turn pulls open the big parachute.

At the top of a parachute there is a small hole through which some of the air trapped under the "umbrella" escapes. The opening helps to steady the fall of a parachute. It lessens the danger of tipping.

Parachutes have to be made of some thin, tough material such as silk or nylon. During World War II there was almost no nylon for clothing. Most of the nylon produced was being used for parachutes. (See AIRPLANES; NYLON; SILK.)

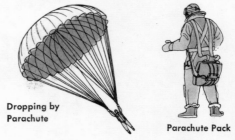

Dropping by Parachute

Parachute Pack

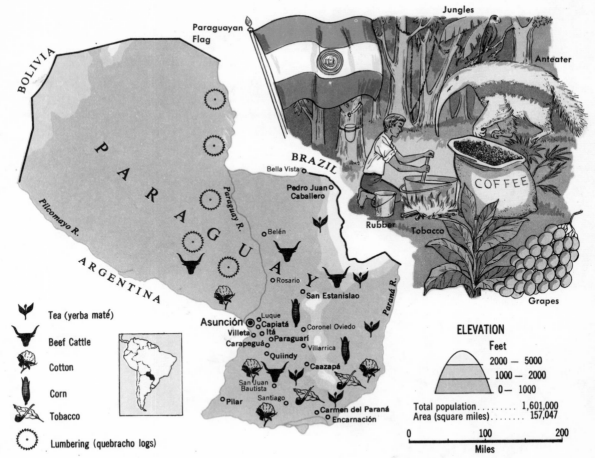

Tea (yerba maté)

Beef Cattle

Cotton

Corn

Tobacco

Lumbering (quebracho logs)

ELEVATION
Feet
2000 — 5000
1000 — 2000
0 — 1000

Total population........ 1,601,000
Area (square miles)........ 157,047

0          100          200
Miles

**PARAGUAY** Two of the 13 countries of South America have no seacoast. They are Paraguay and its neighbor, Bolivia.

Paraguay is a country of forests and grasslands. It has long, hot summers, warm winters, and much rain. Many kinds of crops will grow there. But only one out of every 100 acres is farmed.

Most Paraguayans are part Spanish and part Indian, and speak an Indian language called Guarani. But, especially in the cities, many speak Spanish. Most of the farmers still have only very simple tools.

Wars between Paraguay and its neighbors have hindered progress there. A river route links it with Buenos Aires. But most Paraguayans have had little chance to see modern ways of farming. Asunción, Paraguay's capital, is its only large city. It is a river port, now reached by river steamer, by train, and by plane.

Tourists who visit Asunción enjoy seeing on its streets automobiles and trucks side by side with oxcarts and trains of donkeys. And the city has many lovely homes, churches, and government buildings.

Many cattle are raised in the grasslands. From quebracho trees in the forest, very hard lumber is cut. The name "quebracho" means "ax breaker." An extract made from the wood is used in tanning leather. Among the exports are quebracho, hides, cotton, tobacco, and yerba maté. A drink is made from leaves of yerba maté plants. Some of those plants and some orange trees grow wild in Paraguay.

Paraguay has far fewer people than its smaller neighbor, Uruguay. But several thousand newcomers have settled in Paraguay in recent years. The government is helping in several ways to speed progress there. (See BUENOS AIRES; URUGUAY.)

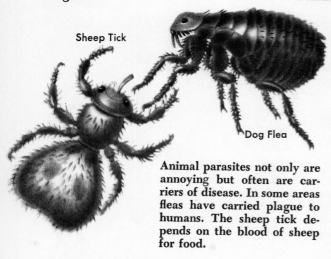

Sheep Tick

Dog Flea

Animal parasites not only are annoying but often are carriers of disease. In some areas fleas have carried plague to humans. The sheep tick depends on the blood of sheep for food.

**PARASITES** A parasite is a plant or animal that lives in or on some other living thing and gets food from it. "Parasite" comes from the Latin for "beside food."

The plant or animal that supports a parasite is called a "host." A parasite's host may have to be a certain kind of living thing. For example, beechdrops, a plant parasite, can live only on the roots of beech trees. Other parasites follow the old saying that "beggars cannot be choosers." It makes no difference to a wood tick, for instance, whether it gets a meal from a man or a dog. Many kinds of dodder will grow on any green plant within reach.

In the course of their lives some parasites have to have more than one host. The tiny one-celled animal that causes malaria must spend part of its life inside a human being and part inside a mosquito.

Many parasites get shelter as well as food from their hosts. A tapeworm lives its whole life inside the body of the animal it gets food from. A flea does not live inside the dog that furnishes it with food, but the dog's thick hair shelters it.

A parasite may not stay with its host all the time. A wood tick ready for a meal crawls up on a small plant. It clings to some animal that brushes against it. It pushes its beak into the skin of the animal and begins filling itself with blood. Perhaps for as long as a week it rides about, taking in as much blood as it can hold. Then it drops off into the grass to digest its big meal.

Some living things are only partial parasites. Mistletoe is one. It perches high on trees and sends roots into them. But it takes nothing but water from the trees. It can make the rest of its food with its leaves.

In the plant kingdom the biggest number of parasites is found in the group called the "fungi." By no means all fungi are parasites, but many are. Much harm is done to both plants and animals by such fungus parasites as rusts and disease bacteria.

In the animal kingdom the parasites are scattered among many groups. There are worms, insects, mites and ticks, tiny animals called protozoa, and others besides.

Being a parasite is not at all an unusual way of getting a living. No large plant or animal escapes having parasites. Most small plants and animals have parasites, too. As a rule, even a parasite is a host to still smaller parasites. A flea, for example, sucks the blood of a dog. In the flea's body there are likely to be some tiny worms. In the bodies of the worms there are likely to be some tiny one-celled animals. And inside these tiny animals there are likely to be bacteria. The jingle which says that "big fleas have little fleas upon their backs to bite 'em" is true. (See BACTERIA; DISEASE GERMS; FUNGI; MISTLETOE.)

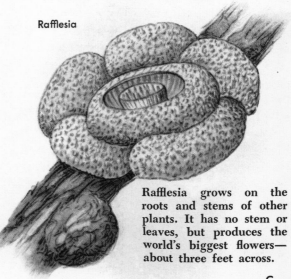

Rafflesia

Rafflesia grows on the roots and stems of other plants. It has no stem or leaves, but produces the world's biggest flowers—about three feet across.

C

# THE GOLDEN BOOK ENCYCLOPEDIA
## CONTAINS THE FOLLOWING VOLUMES

## CONTRIBUTING ARTISTS

Dot and Sy Barlowe • Cornelius De Witt • E. Joseph Dreany • Bruno Frost
James Gordon Irving • Beth and Joe Krush • Harry Lazarus • Andre LeBlanc
H. Charles McBarron • Denny McMains • Harry McNaught
Ray Perlman • John Polgreen • Evelyn Urbanowich

Pauline Batchelder Adams • George Avison • Barry Bart • Ernie Barth • Charles Bellow
Eric Bender • Juanita Bennett • Merrit Berger • Robert D. Bezucha • William Bolin
Thelma Bowie • Matilda Breuer • S. Syd Brown • Peter Buchard • Louise Fulton Bush
Jim Caraway • Nino Carbe • Sam Citron • Gordon Clifton • Mel Crawford • Robert Doremus
Harry Daugherty • Rachel Taft Dixon • Olive Earle • Sydney F. Fletcher • F. Beaumont Fox
Rudolf Freund • Tibor Gergely • Douglas Gorsline • Hamilton Greene • Gerald Gregg
Marjorie Hartwell  •  Hans H. Helweg  •  Janice Holland  •  W. Ben Hunt
Arch and Miriam Hurford • Harper Johnson • Norman Jonsson • Matthew Kalmenoff
Janet Robson Kennedy • Paul Kinnear • Olga Kucera • Walter Kumme • John Leone
Kenneth E. Lowman • John Alan Maxwell • Jean McCammack • Shane Miller • Stina Nagel
Elizabeth Newhall • Gregory Orloff • Raymond Pease • Alice and Martin Provensen
Jerry Robinson  •  Feodor Rojankovsky  •  Roki  •  Mary Royt  •  Arnold W. Ryan
Arthur Sanford  •  Sam Savitts  •  William Sayles  •  Al Schmidt  •  Edwin Schmidt
Frederick E. Seyfarth  •  Robert Sherman  •  George Solonewitsch  •  Lionel Stern
Norton Stewart • Valerie Swenson • Gustaf Tenggren • William Thompson • Felix Traugott
Eileen Fox Vaughn  •  Herschel Wartik  •  Robert Weisman  •  Garth Williams

## MAPS BY

Vincent Kotschar    Jean Paul Tremblay
Carol Vinall    Frederic Lorenzen
Rudolf von Siegl    Francis Barkoczy

## COVER ARTISTS

Ned Seidler • Ken Davies • Don Moss